cooking
by numbers

From eating alone to the more the merrier
– inspired ideas for any occasion

matthew fort

First published in Great Britain in 2007 by
Virgin Books Ltd
Thames Wharf Studios
Rainville Road
London
W6 9HA

A catalogue record for this book is available from the British Library.

ISBN 978 0 7535 1259 3

The paper used in this book is a natural, recyclable product made
from wood grown in sustainable forests. The manufacturing process
conforms to the regulations of the country of origin.

Designed by Design Culture

Illustrations © Barking Dog Art Design and Illustration

Printed and bound in Great Britain by Mackays

contents

introduction

You come in from work at the end of a gruelling day at the coalface. You take off your coat and hang it up, do a head count of the children, pour yourself a glass of something, a little ritual that truly marks the end of the working and commuting day. And then what? Hope that someone else has decided what to have for supper? Grope in the deep freeze for industrial pizza or a plastic box of chicken korma with its deeply seductive packaging? Search high and low for the menu from that new take-away on the high street? Or pluck an onion from the wire rack in the corner, peel off its skin, begin chopping with a firm, decisive hand and start cooking?

This book is for people who like cooking. You may not necessarily cook every day. You may have to fit those kitchen-therapy sessions into a life crowded by work, being the in-house taxi service to your children in their giddy social lives, monthly book-club get-togethers, five-a-side football training sessions, salsa evenings, guitar lessons and all the other distractions of modern life.

Nevertheless, in all this hurly-burly, there is an insistent voice that calls out to get into the kitchen. It's that very modern mixture of guilt and pleasure that prods at our conscience – yes, we ought to, it's good for us, for our families, for our health and actually, it's not that painful when you get down to it. No. Actually, it's (deep breath) – fun. Fun? Yes it is. It's a pretty good feeling, cooking.

And so, when you do have the time and you do finally settle down to the process that begins by peeling and chopping an onion and ends several hours later with a happy sense of repletion and the warm appreciation of your friends or family, dare I suggest that it speaks to a better, deeper part of ourselves. There is nothing, absolutely nothing quite like the pleasure of feeding people who appreciate what we have done for them.

Well, that's the idea, anyway.

It has always seemed to me that what we cook, how we cook and when we cook is dictated by outside circumstances. We don't cook the same way for just one as we do for just two, let alone eight people. When we want to show off our cooking skills at a dinner party for friends, we go about it differently from the way we do if it's a quick snack for all the family.

And it's not just a matter of who and how many we're cooking for, but how much time we have for thinking, planning, shopping and preparation. On the whole most people don't have the time on a day-to-day basis to devote hours to the business of getting a meal together. Both partners in most relationships now work, either by choice or in order to maintain a particular standard of living. If you've been out chiselling a living in a pitiless world all day, it's not easy to have the discipline or energy to settle down to even light kitchen action when you get home.

There's no point in being sanctimonious about this, or going into finger-wagging mode. There is a tendency about some cookery books these days to present home cooking as some kind of moral crusade. These worthy works tend to leave me feeling derelict in my kitchen duty because I haven't cooked rigorously by the seasons, sought out the finest artisanal producers, kept up to date with issues of sustainability, ethical production, chemical residue levels and a whole raft of other concerns.

I am a simple chap. I like cooking. I have always liked cooking. I like to cook every day if I can. That's easy for me now because I get paid to do it, but even when I didn't get paid, I did. In a way it was even easier then. I worked in advertising in those days, and when I got home, I found that cooking was a form of therapy. If I chopped that onion without concentrating, I tended to add slivers of fingertip to the vegetable slices. By concentrating on the physical activity of cooking, I was able to block out the trivia that clogs the mind at the end of the working day – 'Oh God, what are we going to say to the client tomorrow when the ads aren't ready.' 'What did Phil say to David that made him burst into tears?' Stuff like that.

More than that, I found food a therapy while I was at work, too. It seems to me that much of working life in any sector of industry is given over to meetings. 'I'm in a meeting,' we say in a tone of self-importance. In fact meetings are a form of displacement activity, providing the conditions in which people can witter on and on and on, usually repeating what someone else has just wittered on and on and on about. If you are lucky, 3 per cent of time spent in any meeting is actually positive, creative and useful.

So what do you do with the other 97 per cent? You plan the next meal that you're going to cook. That's what I used to do. 'If I put this with that, and then add that . . . On the other hand I could . . .' Or I would sort out my shopping schedule - the butcher and cheese shop during lunch, and then pop into the greengrocer or supermarket on the way home. When I actually got into the kitchen I knew what I was going to do and how I was going to do it and could get stuck in right away. Half an hour, 45 minutes, sometimes 60 minutes later, there it was, supper for two, supper for four, dinner for six or whatever.

OK, so my career in advertising wasn't exactly stellar, but I learned a lot about cooking and I had a good deal of fun and I kept my friends and family happy. That's what it's all about at the end of the day. And in the middle of the day, too.

1. not exactly cutting edge

My kitchen

It is axiomatic that the kitchen has yet to be built that has enough surface area to hold all the equipment, gadgets and general clutter that any cook inevitably acquires, and still leave enough to work on. Kitchen equipment seems to breed invisibly, expanding to take all the space available. When I actually come to do any cooking, it always seems to involve moving stuff from here to there, clearing this area to make way for that, and then moving that to fit in something else. And there always comes a point when I wander around with a red-hot pan gradually burning its way through my oven gloves, trying to find somewhere to put the damn thing down.

My kitchen is probably larger than most. It is fourteen feet by twelve feet. It is filled with light from windows facing south and west. Down one side runs a long beech surface, with the sink set into it. This is where the CD player, toaster, draining racks, kettle and microwave – yes, I do have one – sit, along with a load of other clutter that naturally accumulates in kitchens: phone, container of dried bread, things to hold washing-up brushes, sponges, tins containing tea and chocolate, half-drunk bottles of wine, etc., etc. One window occupies the end wall, with a table between it and the other window on the next wall. This is where we sit to eat. I hate that table for all its practicality. It is so ugly that I insist on hiding it beneath a tablecloth at all times.

Then comes the cooker, fitted into what used to be a chimney breast. It's a big beast, a cream-coloured Falcon with two ovens for cooking, a decent grill and a warming oven, and five hobs. It is very solid, very heavy and very reliable and I love it to bits, even when I have to clean it.

Above the cooker is a shelf loaded with Kilner jars in which I store nuts, oatmeal, chillies, demerara sugar and muesli. To the right of the cooker is a small table with a set of shelves above it. These hold all the oils, vinegars and other flavouring agents I use in cooking. I will list these in greater detail shortly.

Then there is a door to the garden and the whole of the end wall is occupied with a dresser with an ingenious system of slats from which dangle pots and pans. Below them, on the flat surface, stand various bits of equipment, and in the cupboards below them are all manner of bowls, with saucepan lids and spices held in two sea-grass baskets.

Finally, in the middle of the kitchen, between the cooker and the sink, stands a medium-sized chopping table that has been a good friend for a great many years. On it I do most of my work. Below it is a bin for collecting vegetable parings for the compost heap and another sea-grass basket containing ingredients for making Auntie Mary's super soda bread, the only bread I regularly bake because of its extreme simplicity. And that's it – nothing grand, nothing fancy, nothing designed for posing; just cooking.

My equipment

I am not a gadget fanatic. All you really need to start with is a knife, a pan and a source of heat. It's amazing what you can cook when you are forced to pare your equipment down to essentials. I have had several memorable meals cooked over a wood fire, using chicken wire as a grill, with just a frying pan in support.

Having said that, oh yes, I have accumulated loads of stuff over the years. In fact there is a drawer so stuffed with oyster openers, patent peelers, variations on a corkscrew and other bits of metal whose use, frankly, I have forgotten, that it frequently jams when I try to open it.

However, there is plenty of equipment that I love. I'm not suggesting for a moment that you need all of it or even any of it. It's just stuff that I find useful.

Knives

I have two big chef's knives, one stainless steel, the other carbon; a broad-bladed, stainless-steel Japanese vegetable knife with ingenious holes down the side that stop whatever I am cutting from sticking to the blade; a shorter chef's knife that my wife prefers to use; a bread knife; and two small paring knives. These all live in a slit at the back of the chopping table along with a steel and an old-fashioned corkscrew.

In a drawer beneath there are: a fish-filleting knife; a boning knife; an ultra-sharp Japanese paring knife; a short, heavy Japanese fish-filleting knife; a knife for filleting eels, not much used; and two huge Chinese cleavers.

Pans

I have five frying pans and a griddle pan. This may seem excessive. It may even be excessive, but I use them all. Three are cast iron, and were part of the dowry that my wife brought to our marriage. The griddle pan, so useful for giving those desirable black lines on griddled bread, chops, skirt steak and other ingredients, is also cast iron. Then there are two nonstick frying pans, one large and one small. Around them are ranged seven saucepans of varying shapes and sizes, including one nonstick, one used only for boiling eggs and one used only for making my porridge in. There's a steamer, two casseroles, two stockpots, a wok-ish thing and a big stainless-steel sauté pan. They all have one thing in common. They have thick bases to distribute the heat evenly.

Electrical equipment

I am a great believer in saving as much labour as I can. On the other hand, I also follow the Italian principle that certain jobs are better done by hand when the nature of the action can materially affect the quality of the dish. Chopping is a case in point. With very few exceptions, I chop everything by hand because chopping in a food processor tends to: a) produce bits of varying sizes, which makes for uneven cooking; and b) also smashes liquid out of anything being chopped, vegetables in particular.

Having said that, of course I have a food processor, which gets a fair amount of use. Beside it is a Kenwood Chef, of which I am very fond. I use this for mixing, purées, mincing and making sausages.

In another room is an ice-cream machine. It is in another room because, while it makes very fine ice cream and sorbets, I find that its laborious stirring sounds rather grate on the ear after a while.

There is a microwave, too, about which I am deeply ambivalent. My wife and daughter infiltrated it into the house when I wasn't looking. It is fine for part-cooking baked potatoes (which I finish off in the oven), cooking squashes (although you have to be careful that they don't explode, pebble-dashing the inside of the machine which is absolutely bloody to clean), and defrosting stock. That's not a lot.

Finally, I have an electric hand-beater, which is essential. And that's about it. Of course I am thinking about getting a couple of other bits of electronic wizardry, but I haven't got round to it yet. Just as well, because I haven't got the space.

Other essential bits and bobs

Meat thermometer Absolutely essential if you don't want to have to do those challenging mental calculations every time you cook a piece of meat. It may be because I took five attempts to pass Maths GCSE (or O level as it was in those days), but I prefer to just stick my thermometer into the meat in question, and it tells me whether or not it is cooked. None of that twenty minutes a pound at 200°C/ 400°F/Gas 6 for the first hour and then fifteen minutes a pound at 180°F/350°C/Gas 4 for the next two hours, which always made my head ache.

Oven thermometer It always helps to know whether your principle bit of cooking machinery is working properly. Built-in thermostats are notoriously unreliable. A good oven thermometer helps take some of the uncertainty out of roasting and baking.

Mandolin For very thin slicing, i.e. fennel for salads, carrots for stews, cabbage for, well, heaps of things. I would very much like to be able to afford a proper, gleaming, stainless-steel job, but the excellent cutting blade set into a sturdy plastic frame seems to work very well for me.

Tongs Almost my favourite piece of kitchen equipment. For turning over sizzling chops, lifting a roasting chicken out of its pan, flipping over strips of bacon, picking up bits of food from the floor so that I don't have to bend over too far. Those tongs get more use than anything other than my knives.

Grater I have a thing about graters. I used to think that all the high-design products you get in kitchen catalogues don't seem to work as well as the old-fashioned boxy thing with a handle on the top, fine grating on one side, coarse grating on the other, peel grater at one end. And then I bought a set of extremely expensive micro-graters and my life changed. Or my view of graters did.

Potato ricer Looks like a medieval instrument of torture. Of course, it isn't essential to have a potato ricer, but it does help make the best mash and the best potato gnocchi. And riced potato makes a sophisticated change from straight mash, too.

On the Shelf

That is, the shelf to the right-hand side of the cooker.

Oils

General-purpose extra-virgin olive oil for cooking. The oil
is full of character, often quite peppery. These characteristics
will modify or disappear altogether during cooking. I buy this
in five-litre tins and top up the rather shapely bottle with
a pour spout.

Special extra-virgin olive oil for vinaigrettes, dribbling over
vegetables or bruschetta. There may be one or two bottles
depending on whim. I prefer smooth, mellow, un-peppery,
fruity oils for this.

A bottle of peanut oil for some frying duties and for particular
vinaigrettes (e.g. mustardy dressings for artichokes and chicory).
Peanut oil has a high burning point and, to my palate, a higher
viscosity than most other oils, which means it clings to surfaces
in a particularly seductive way.

A random selection of other oils that I pick up in the spirit of
discovery or that have been sent to me. At the moment they
include argon oil, avocado oil, sesame oil and olive oil infused
with lemon.

Vinegars

I am something of a vinegar anorak. Currently I have seven
ordinary wine vinegars: two chardonnays, a cabernet sauvignon,
an old French red, two sherry, and a vinegar I make myself of
leftover wines of every colour and variety. Then there are three
cider vinegars, walnut vinegar, rice-wine vinegar, three proper
balsamic vinegars, fig balsamic, apple balsamic and a few odds
and ends.

I love this range. For a start, vinegars are immensely versatile. They make significant differences to hot and cold dishes as well as vinaigrettes. You can add them at the beginning, the middle or at the end of making a dish, and they will have a different impact at each stage. The effect they will have depends on their own character. Some are fierce and assertive, some are gentle and refined, and still others tread the middle ground, as it were. So you can vary the qualities of your vinaigrettes, for example, depending on the ingredients of the salad, whim or mood.

Other bottles

Firstly, there are the alcoholic helpers: Chambery vermouth for dishes and sauces needing white wine if I don't have a bottle of white wine open; Noilly Prat for particular fish dishes; marsala, one of my favourites, which goes into any number of game and meat dishes; white port and red port, which both lay down firm foundations for many sauces. Vino cotto – grape must, which has been greatly reduced – is useful for boosting some Italian dishes.

Then there are the more or less nonalcoholic flavour enhancers as well: angostura bitters; Tabasco sauce; Worcestershire sauce; mirin, a nice, well-behaved, slightly sweet Japanese condiment derived from rice; tamari; soya sauce; and nam pla or Thai fish sauce, which adds a bit of oomph to sauces or dressings that need it.

All of these will crop up from time to time in the recipes.

Recipes

My cooking is firmly in what you might call the European mainstream, that is a chunk of British, a slosh of French and a dash of Italian. I do try the odd sally into the sunny uplands of Indian, Asian and oriental cooking, but my heart isn't really in it. It's a failing, I know, but no one's really complained. Yet. Some of these recipes have appeared in the *Weekend Guardian*, but only a few.

As the title of the book suggests, the recipes have been devised for particular numbers of eaters. If you find a recipe you like the sound of, but want to cook it for a different number of people, just multiply or divide accordingly. You know you can do it really. The recipes have been arranged in ascending order of elaboration. Those in the sections headed 'A Piece of Cake' are dead simple, quick 'n' easy. Those in the 'No Sweat' section are probably just as quick and easy, but need a touch more attention. 'Making an Effort' means what it says, although, in reality, the recipes are not that complicated. They just mean that your guests who eat them will really appreciate the work that you've put in.

Suppliers

I remember looking at this John Dory for a long time. Its eye was bright and clear. I lifted up the gill cover, expecting the fishmonger to bark at me at any moment, but he didn't. The gill itself was a vivid claret red. There was a firmness and sheen to its flat, mottled side. It smelled clean, as if it had just swum in from the sea. I bought it, and had the fishmonger fillet it, keeping the bones to make the stock that would make the sauce that . . .

I bought the John Dory because I had fallen in love with it, in a kind of way. That may seem bonkers, and I suppose it is. It was only a fish, after all. But it excited my imagination. It started off an interior conversation about how I would cook it, what would go with it. It made me want to cook it. I could sense the firm, sweet, meaty fillet in my mouth already. I could feel the first stirrings of pleasure. That's what good ingredients can do for you, or do for me at any rate.

So from the fishmongers it was a short hop to the farm shop for asparagus and new Cornish potatoes and little carrots. There's no point in doing a dozen vegetables, in my view, when two or three at the top of their game will do the job and not clutter up the flavours. And from there to the supermarket. Yes. Why not?

There's good unsalted butter for cream, and I like to get my Chambery vermouth that I prefer to wine for making fish sauces. And I can satisfy my occasional cravings for fruit-and-nut chocolate. And then it was on to . . .

The point I'm trying to make is that good food starts with good ingredients, and ends with good ingredients. It's possible to make OK food with OK ingredients, but to make good food you need good ingredients, and to make the best food you need the best ingredients. It's quite simple. There's nothing very original about any of this, but it seems to me that it's worth stating first principles from time to time. You can, of course, make bad food with the best ingredients, but that's another matter.

And the second point is that you get good, and the best, ingredients from the most resourceful and responsible of suppliers, suppliers who know and care passionately about what they serve.

I am extraordinarily fortunate. In the area of Gloucestershire in which I live – around Stroud, if you're looking for somewhere to move – there's a masterly fishmonger in one village (who has a line or two in classy non-fish produce from hither and yon, too) as well as a very good fish stall in town on a Friday; two top-notch butchers; farm shops aplenty; an ace baker; Michael, the winter veg man; and one of the best farmer's markets in the country. It is quite possible to shop locally and seasonally all year and eat as well as anyone in the country. It turns shopping into a treasure hunt.

I have identified these suppliers and appointed them (unofficially) as purveyors of fine foods to the Fort household through a long period of trial and error. In the process, I identified the following base criteria for choosing them:

1. Quality and freshness of produce. The secret to a successful food shop is turnover. I'm sure the same is true for any shop of any kind, but it has particular pertinence as far as food is concerned because of the perishable nature of the goods.

The faster the foodstuffs fly out the shop, the fresher the stuff coming in will be.

2. Humanity, liberality, abundance, buy-me, eat-me. Why is it that you can go to a supermarket, spend £50 on food and come out feeling depressed? And go to a market, spend £100 on food and walk out with a spring in your step, your head buzzing with ideas and a feeling that life is worth living after all? A good food shop, market, supplier, should have that second effect on you. It comes from display, from the art of generosity, from making you feel that you matter to them.

3. Service. Part of this sense of wellbeing comes from the very simple matter of human contact. A good supplier will look at you, talk to you, answer your questions, and remember who you are the next time you go in. They should be happy to spend time instructing you in the finer points of whatever it is you're buying.

4. Expertise. That's why you're going there. The supplier is an expert, or should be. They should be able and happy to answer your questions, no matter how daft they may seem to be.

5. Checking, testing, tasting. The modern fad for packaging makes it almost impossible to examine what you're buying properly. It seems ironic that almost the last place you can actually examine fruit and veg, and choose your own, is in the supermarket. But a good supplier should let you do that, and even let you nibble on the produce by way of reassuring you of its quality. How often have I been into a deli or market or whatever in France or Italy, and been handed a sliver of cheese, a slice of sausage, or a strawberry or cherry to test? It's simple salesmanship.

And once you have decided who is going to be your meat supplier, baker, fruit-and-veg person or whatever, talk to them. Think how flattered you are when someone takes an interest in what you do. They are no different. We all like showing off our expertise, experience and judgement. A butcher, a fishmonger is no different.

And ask questions. Where does this lamb come from? What's the breed? How long has it been hung for? And don't worry about looking a fool. You're a fool if you don't ask questions. There's no virtue in pretending to know about something when you don't. More importantly, it's an essential part of the process of deciding where you're going to spend your money. If they can't be bothered to deal with you decently, then take your business elsewhere.

And above all, don't be afraid to complain. Once I said to the proprietor of the restaurant in which I was eating, who was also a friend, that the fish I had just finished had been overcooked. The next thing I knew, he had grabbed me by the throat and pinned me to the wall. What on earth was the point, he demanded, of telling him now, when I had eaten all the evidence? I should have said something at the time. It was a fair point. We don't complain nearly enough in this country. But be reasonable and reasoned about it. Don't ask for your money back (unless you feel you've been taken for a serious ride). I find the more-in-sorrow-than-in-anger works best. If they dispute your claims and doubt your veracity, just nod quietly, leave, and then advise everyone you meet what stupid gits they are.

And finally, keep reviewing your suppliers. You should wake each morning expecting to eat the very best food there is to be had. You deserve nothing less.

not exactly cutting edge | 21

2. cooking for one

OK, OK, OK. Yes, I've done it too – had the baked beans on toast, with or without a fried egg or a rasher or two of crisp bacon. And I've eaten them cold out of the tin. With a silver spoon. Some decencies have to be preserved. And I'm pretty keen on sardines on toast, mashed, sprinkled with salt, dashed with lemon juice and overlaid with thin slices of cucumber as a light lunchtime nibble. And I'm partial to sarnies of various hues, too, and pork pies and cold sausages all have their attractions and joys when I'm on my own.

There's no shame in it. We all have to do it sooner or later. Eat on your own, that is. In fact, there are many things to recommend it – having the kitchen and house to yourself, and not having to negotiate over the menu, when you eat or choice of TV programme for a start.

Still, I don't believe that only having to cater for yourself is always an excuse to let your standards slip. More than that, there is pleasure in the careful ritual of preparing food, in treating yourself, in trying out new ideas, in cooking things you don't get a chance to when you're cooking for the rest of the family or friends. And you don't have to be so exacting either. I think we can all put up with a certain sloppiness or inattention to detail when it's only us who'll be eating.

And even if you don't get that uplifting round of applause that may be yours when you cook for others, there's no chance of the brickbats either. As Oscar Wilde should have said, 'Falling in love with your own cooking is the beginning of a lifelong romance that knows no disappointments.'

I am assuming, by the way, that none of us is so sad that we would make a pudding as well as a proper plateful. A bit of cheese, a helping of fruit, something like that should be quite enough. All right, finish off the day before yesterday's tart, if you must, or raid that tub of pecan-fudge-chocolate-chip-butterscotch-blow-the-diet tub of ice cream.

❧ a piece of cake ❧

Chicken Livers and Lettuce with a Warm Soft-boiled Egg

Chicken livers – cheap, cheerful, tasty. What more do you want? I like the soft-boiled egg touch because I like soft-boiled eggs, and the idea of the chicken (well, part of it) forming an alliance with its egg has a pleasing holistic touch.

1 chicken's egg (or 2 if you're greedy)
enough salad for 1
(Little Gem is fine; romaine will do; Frisee is best of all)
extra-virgin olive oil
juice of ¼ lemon

balsamic vinegar
170g fresh chicken livers
¼ tsp ground cumin
¼ tsp ground star anise
¼ tsp ground white pepper
salt
55g butter

1. Boil the egg for 4 minutes. Peel when cool enough.

2. Wash the lettuce, dry thoroughly, tear up and put in a bowl.

3. Dress with olive oil, lemon juice and balsamic vinegar to your liking (I suggest 60 per cent oil, 20 per cent lemon juice, 20 per cent balsamic vinegar) and season.

4. Mix all the spices together and roll the chicken livers in them, making sure that they are well coated.

5. Heat the butter in a frying pan until foaming.

6. Toss in the livers and cook for 2 to 3 minutes. I like them pink and juicy. If you like them not quite so pink, cook them for a little longer, but be careful not to overcook them or they will go nasty and grainy. Season with salt.

7. Plonk them on top of the salad.

8. Cut the egg(s) in half and place enticingly where you think best.

Pork Kebab with Sweet and Sour Cabbage and Carrot Salad

Light, fresh, clean-tasting. Who could ask for more?

1 dried red chilli
1 lime
1 dsp caster sugar
¼ white cabbage
1 or 2 carrots
1 tsp mustard seed
200g pork bits (fillet, or whatever)
peanut oil
salt and pepper

1. Finely chop the chilli and put in a bowl with the juice of the lime and the sugar. Stir until the sugar is dissolved.

2. Finely shred the cabbage and the carrot(s).

3. Mix them with the dressing.

4. Heat the mustard seeds in a frying pan until they begin to pop.

5. Distribute them over the cabbage and carrot salad.

6. Cut the pork into small, bite-sized cubes.

7. Heat the oil in a frying pan until very hot.

8. Brown the pork on all sides, season with salt and pepper and arrange on top of the salad.

There's no mystery or great effort to making risotto, and it's a good deal quicker than some books would let you believe. I adapted this from a dish I had just outside Mantua. Unless I have stock, usually chicken, standing by, I pour a tablespoon of good commercial chicken stock into the saucepan after the rice and then add boiling water from the kettle. That's when it's just for me. I'll do it properly when I want to impress other people.

1 small onion
100g pork sausage meat (or sausages chopped up)
100g back bacon
30g butter
1 tbsp vegetable oil
50g arborio rice
200ml stock
1 tbsp chopped parsley
1 dsp freshly grated Parmesan (optional)
salt and pepper

1. Chop the onion, slice the sausages and cut the bacon into thick matchsticks.

2. Heat the oil and butter in a saucepan.

3. When they are foaming, toss in the onion, bacon and sausage pieces. Fry until the fat runs from the bacon and the onion is translucent.

4. Pour in the rice and turn over in the fat.

5. Add the stock bit by bit, stirring as often as you can manage. We are not making a textbook risotto here, but the more you stir, the more starch you release from the rice.

6. After 15 minutes test the rice. It will probably need a little more cooking.

7. Off the heat, beat in the chopped parsley and grated Parmesan (if using) or other cheese, if you like. Season with salt and plenty of black pepper.

Cider, Cheese 'n' Ham on Toast

Of course good cheese is best eaten on its own in its natural state, perhaps with an apple to go with it, such as Ashmead's Kernel, Ellison's Orange or St Edmond's Pippin. But if you have a hunk that's past its prime, then this kind of anglicised croque monsieur is as good a way of finishing it as any. And the cider adds the health-giving touch of apple. Sort of.

400g grated cheese
150ml sweet cider
½ tsp English mustard
several dashes of Worcestershire sauce
2 slices of buttered toast
freshly ground pepper

1. Grate the cheese into a saucepan.

2. Add the cider, mustard and Worcestershire sauce and bring to the boil.

3. Turn down the heat to very low and stir, stir, stir until the cheese has melted and the cider been absorbed and you have a smooth, cheesy cream. Grind in plenty of black pepper.

4. Place a slice of ham on top of the buttered toast. Pour the melted cheese on top of that. Slide under the grill until brown and bubbling.

Skirt is that coarse and fibrous flap of meat that covers the rib. Lots of people turn up their noses at it, but not me. It makes a splendid, and cheap, treat for one. And for two, come to that. You can easily adapt the recipe for more, too.

150g beef skirt
salt and pepper

1. Cut the skirt into 4 pieces.

2. With a tenderising mallet or other similar tool – I have used just blocks of wood in the past – bash each piece so that it thins and flattens out. This helps break down the connective tissue in the skirt. It also makes the steaks go further.

3. Heat a griddle pan until smoking (or a frying pan with just a little oil). Place the individual thin skirt steaks in it – you will have to do this in batches.

4. Cook for 1 minute. Turn over. Cook for another minute.

5. Season and serve on a good, thick slice of bread slathered in mustard or the dressing below.

For the dressing
2dsp capers (preferably the salted ones)
2 anchovy fillets
¼ tsp French mustard
juice of 1 lemon
85ml extra-virgin olive oil

1. Rinse the salt off the capers very thoroughly.

2. Place all the ingredients in a blender or food processor and

blend or process until more or less smooth. It doesn't matter if there are a few lumps in this.

3. Spread a thin layer of the dressing onto the skirt when it is on the bread.

Lambs' Kidneys Roasted in their Fat

A dish my mother taught me. Frankly, I never get to eat enough offal. Kidneys, liver, sweetbreads, brain, heart, chitterlings, I love each and every one of them. But one of the reasons I never get to eat enough of it is that not too many people on the domestic front share my passion. So I have to indulge in my hideous vice on my own when there's no one about to go, 'Eeuurrgh. How horrid.' This is the simplest of simple recipes.

2-4 lambs' kidneys in their fat
(you'll only be able to get these from a bona fide butcher)
1-2 slices of toast
salt and pepper

1. Turn on oven to 180°C/350°F/Gas 4.

2. Put kidneys onto a roasting tray.

3. Put into oven.

4. Leave there for 20 minutes.

5. Take out.

6. Peel away fat with a sharp knife.

7. Cut in half and put onto slices of toast.

8. Season. Eat. With mustard if you must, and some undressed watercress if you are looking for a balanced dish.

Peaches in White Wine

No reason why you shouldn't be civilised just because you're on your own. Here's another perfect small indulgence for you (me). Something like prosecco or a sweet wine would do nicely, or even elderflower fizz if you want to be teetotal.

1 very ripe peach
white wine

1. Peel and slice peach and put it into a glass.

2. Pour the wine over it and let it steep for 30 minutes or so.

3. Eat, drink and be happy.

❧ no sweat ❧

Poached Egg on Butter Beans and Ham

I have a thing about butter beans. I quite like them straight from the tin (when no one's looking). They're dead easy to cook from scratch if you buy the dry version (which make, incidentally, a very fine mash, with garlic, olive oil and lemon juice). But as we're on our own tonight, it's time to reach for the can.

1 can of butter beans
85g ham (preferably smoked and cut thick)
30g butter
salt and pepper

2tsp whole-grain mustard
1tbsp chopped parsley
1 fresh egg

1. Drain the liquid off the butter beans.

2. Cut the ham into strips about 0.5cm thick.

3. Melt the butter in a saucepan.

4. Add the ham strips and fry gently for a couple of minutes.
    Add the butter beans and stir round to mix with the ham.

5. Season with salt and plenty of pepper.

6. Put the lid on the saucepan, turn down the heat and
    braise gently for 20 minutes or so.

7. Add chopped parsley and stir in the mustard just
    before serving.

8. Poach the egg.

9. Decant beans 'n' ham to plate. Place egg on top.
    Eat in cheery solitude.

Chicken Slivers with Rocket

This is a home-grown version of a dish I have enjoyed several
times in one of my favourite restaurants in Rome, the Ristorante
Abruzzo. They use beef and no chilli. I'm more likely to have
chicken lying around at home than beef.

85g rocket
115g chicken breast
1 hot red chilli

olive oil
juice of ¼ lemon
salt and pepper

1. Arrange the rocket on a plate.

2. Cut the chicken into thin strips maybe 1cm thick.
    Make sure they are really dry.

3. Dice the chilli finely.

4. Heat the olive oil in a frying pan until smoking.
    Toss in the chilli, followed quickly by the chicken,
    and fry for 1 minute, 2 at most.

5. Sprinkle the chicken slivers over the rocket.

6. Squeeze the lemon juice over the chicken and leaves.
    Season and eat with a chunk of bread and a glass of wine.

making an effort

Scrambled Egg with Roasted Peppers and Anchovies

A kind of piperade (not that the Basques would recognise it).
The finest scrambled egg is the apotheosis of slow food, because
the slower the eggs are scrambled, the better they will be. I know
that I will lose most of my readers at this point, but in my view
scrambled eggs need to be cooked for 40 minutes or more to be at
their best. That means cooking them over the hob equivalent of
a candle. Of course I can't always be bothered with this council
of perfection, although when I do, I attain a kind of Zen-like
sense of tranquillity, and the results are well worth waiting for.

That may be because you have waited for them, but I think you'll find that they have a vastly superior creaminess of texture, as if each fleck of egg had been cooked individually. I like my scrambled eggs to taste of eggs, so no milk or cream in the mix, thank you very much, and this is one dish in which I try to keep butter to a minimum. Sometimes I add herbs, but the blandness of egg works very well with the sharp, intense saltiness of the anchovies and the silky sweetness of the peppers. Very fine for a Sunday evening snack. Toast is optional. I prefer it without.

150g roasted red peppers
1 tsp butter
pepper
3 free-range eggs
2 anchovy fillets

1. Slice the peppers into thin strips.

2. Melt the butter in a saucepan.

3. Take the pan off the heat. Add a few grindings of pepper.

4. Break the eggs into the pan and break up with a wooden spoon.

5. Place back on the hob with the heat turned down as low as possible. Slip your mind into neutral and stir slowly for the next 20 minutes. If the eggs look like becoming solid too quickly, remove from the heat and cool down while still stirring. Continue cooking and stirring, stirring and cooking, until the eggs have achieved a lustrous, creamy solidity.

6. Just before you're ready to eat your perfectly scrambled eggs, chop the anchovies and add them and the peppers; stir in to make sure they are evenly distributed throughout.

Prosciutto, Aubergine, Mozzarella and Tomato Sandwich

A cosmopolitan version of the cheese on toast on page 28.

1 *aubergine*
salt
olive oil
3 *or* 4 *slices prosciutto*
1 *tomato*
115g *mozzarella*
pepper

1. Turn on oven to 180C°/350°F/Gas 4.

2. Slice the aubergine lengthways. Slices should be quite thick –
   1-2cm. You should end up with 3 or 4 slices of aubergine.

3. Salt and leave for 30 minutes. Rinse off the salt and pat dry.

4. Lay the aubergine slices on a baking tray liberally splashed
   with olive oil. Pop into the oven for 10 minutes.

5. Take out and lay 2 slices of prosciutto on each slice of
   aubergine. Slice the tomato and lay that on top of the ham.
   Slice the mozzarella and lay that on top of the tomato.
   Douse with olive oil and grind quite a lot of pepper over it.

6. Pop into the oven for 5 minutes until the aubergine is soft
   and the cheese melted and bubbling.

Duck Breast and Lentils

I always cook lentils in industrial quantities and then use them
or freeze them in batches so when inspiration or supplies are at
a low ebb, hey presto, there's at least the basis for a decent plate
of something.

1 medium carrot
1 small onion
½ stick of celery
115g smoky bacon
1 tbsp vegetable oil
50g small green lentils
1 tbsp cider vinegar
200ml chicken stock
1 duck breast
small bunch of parsley
salt and pepper

1. Dice the carrot, onion, celery and bacon as small as you can.

2. Heat the oil in a saucepan until smoking.

3. Throw in the diced vegetables and the bacon, lower the heat and fry for 10 minutes or so. Add the lentils and the cider vinegar. Turn the vegetables and lentils in the fat and vinegar.

4. Add the stock, turn down the heat and clap a lid on the pot.

5. Shove the duck breast on a cold griddle or underneath the grill.

6. Turn on the heat under the griddle or the grill. The griddle will begin to cook the duck as it heats up. You can see how the breast is cooking through by noting how it changes colour.

7. Turn over after 7 minutes (possibly earlier on the grill, which will cook it quicker – you don't want to burn the breast).

8. You can season it and just pop on top of the lentils or cut it up into bite-size chunklets, and stir into the lentils. It's easier to eat that way.

9. Chop the parsley and add to the mix. Taste it and season accordingly.

Kohl Rabi, Carrot & White Cabbage Salad with Marinated Chicken Breast

A munchy, crunchy kind of dish that makes for easy portion control and easy cooking, and that's the way to go when you're cooking for one. The secret of the salad is to make it in advance and dress it so the cabbage has a chance to soften up a bit.

½ kohl rabi
1 carrot
¼ (or less) white cabbage
2 anchovy fillets (preferably salted)
¼ lemon
4tsp extra-virgin olive oil
½ chicken breast
salt

1. Shred the kohl rabi and carrot into thin strips. I do this with an ingenious hand-held device with razor-sharp teeth that you drag down the vegetable.

2. Slice the cabbage very finely, cutting out any core. Mix all the vegetable strips together.

3. Mash the anchovy fillets into the lemon juice and add the oil. Add a bit more than that specified if you like. Leave for 30 minutes or so.

4. Cook the chicken breast like the duck breast in the previous recipe, seasoning after cooking.

5. After chopping it up into chunklets, squeeze the lemon over the bits, so they absorb the juices as they cool.

3. recipes for two

Cooking for two people is about twenty times more rewarding than cooking for one, even if it's just your mother, brother or the boy/girl next door. I'm tempted to get all whoozy and say it's about giving, sharing and communion, and so it might be. But it's just as much about showing off, of being told what a wonderful person you are, of being showered with those words of praise and appreciation that are so conspicuously lacking in the rest of one's life (well, mine, anyway). It also encourages a bit more thought and display. I mean, you might have a two-course supper if it's a bog-standard week night, or you might be tempted to go for the full three-courser if you're in a wooing mood.

The recipes in this section can either function on their own, on the bowl-of-soup-a-crust-of-bread-and-thou-beside-me-in-the-wilderness principle, quite enough for a Monday evening, or they can be part of a menu that slowly builds through its parts to a triumphant whole (or, alternatively, to snoring your head off in front of Newsnight). There is no reason why you shouldn't mix and match, starting with the Butter Bean, Pancetta and Rosemary Spread while you set about making the Ham, Barley and Swede Soup, progressing to Souped-up Fishcakes and finishing up with cheese and fruit, or even Mashed Bananas with Strawberry Jam and Cream. Go on, spoil yourself. And them.

❧ a piece of cake ❧

Butter Bean, Pancetta and Rosemary Spread

You know the Italians always have a salami kicking around, and cheese and pickled vegetables and good bread so that everyone has something to nibble while they wait for the main events to turn up on the table. Well, this is a version of that idea. Always have something in the fridge that you can assemble quickly and easily to keep the worst pangs of hunger at bay. And, to be absolutely truthful, the spreads in this and other chapters were based on some I had on a farm in Sicily, where all vegetables manage to taste more of themselves than you would think possible.

1 onion
125g pancetta
1 tbsp extra-virgin olive oil
2 cloves garlic
235g cooked butter beans (400g tin)
100ml chicken or vegetable stock
1 decent sprig rosemary
salt and pepper

1. Peel and finely dice the onion and pancetta.

2. Pour the olive oil into a saucepan. Heat and add the onion and pancetta. Fry until soft and translucent.

3. Add the garlic, butter beans and stock. Cook gently for about 15 minutes.

4. Take off the heat and add the rosemary. Let it cool. Take out the rosemary and mash.

5. Season with salt and pepper, and maybe just a little more
   olive oil.

Broccoli and Anchovy Spread

1 clove garlic
1 small red dried chilli
4 anchovy fillets
1tbsp extra-virgin olive oil
200g broccoli
salt and pepper
juice of ½ lemon

1. Finely chop the garlic, chilli and anchovy fillets.
   Fry in a saucepan with 1tbsp olive oil.

2. When the garlic begins to turn gold, roughly chop and
   add the broccoli. Add 100ml water and simmer until
   the broccoli is soft.

3. Mash, season with salt and pepper and then add the
   lemon juice.

Ham, Barley and Swede Soup

It was a day that called for something hearty and comforting.
The rain was sluicing down outside. The wind was hammering
at the windows. I knew there was the tag end of a knuckle of
ham lurking about somewhere, and some swedes that needed
using up. And there was my old friend, the packet of barley.
Barley tends to get bypassed in favour of more modish lentils
or fancy beans (see coco on page 51) or exotic visitors such
as quinoa, but my tummy has a very soft spot for the mild-
mannered, ever-reliable barley.

25g barley
1 litre ham stock
200g cooked ham
1 onion
1 swede
2tbsp vegetable oil (not olive oil)
or (better still) dripping, lard or duck fat
salt and pepper

1. Put the barley into a saucepan and pour in the stock.

2. Bring to the boil and simmer gently until the barley is cooked – maybe 45 minutes to an hour.

3. Dice the ham and the vegetables not too finely. In another pan heat the vegetable oil or melt the fat.

4. Add the diced vegetables. Stir around until well coated with the warm oil/fat.

5. Cook for about 3 or 4 minutes.

6. Add the barley and stock and cook for another 7 or 8 minutes. Check for seasoning and adjust accordingly.

Watercress, Potatoes, Duck Eggs and Pancetta Salad

Except for gulls' eggs (which have a blink-and-you-miss-it season as well as an eye-watering price) duck eggs make the best hard-boiled eggs in my view. And teamed up with good potatoes, peppery watercress and crisp bacon, they make for a humdinger of a salad.

4 medium-sized waxy potatoes
(e.g. pink fir apple, nicola, charlotte, belle de fontenay)
1 orange

8 slices of pancetta
4 duck eggs (or chicken or 12 quails' eggs)
2 clumps of watercress

1. Peel and dice the potatoes and cook in salted boiling water until cooked through but still holding their shape and texture.

2. Drain and roll immediately in the dressing below and leave to cool.

3. Peel the orange and cut out the individual segments from their surrounding casing. Put them into a bowl with the potato bits.

4. Fry the slices of pancetta until crisp and brown. Put on kitchen towel, drain and cool.

5. Cook the duck eggs in boiling water for about 10 minutes until hard.

6. Cool in cold water, peel and quarter.

7. Break up the watercress and plop into the bowl. Turn them over in the dressing making sure the potato bits and orange segments haven't all sunk to the bottom. Position the egg quarters to nice effect. Break up pancetta slices and scatter over the top.

Dressing

You may have your own way of making dressings, and I am sure they will work just as well as mine. In fact, I tend to alter mine, usually through the choice of vinegar – I keep about eight on permanent stand-by – according to whim, mood or the inspiration of the moment. But I do like to have a higher oil content than is classically allowed. And the amount of salt is also very important.

½ tsp Dijon mustard
juice of 1 orange
10dsp extra-virgin olive oil
½ tsp salt
pepper

Put everything into a jar and shake it up to get it all properly
mixed, or mix it in the serving dish, adding the orange juice to
the mustard and getting that well mixed before adding the oil.
The mustard helps emulsify the other ingredients (or does
it make a colloid? I am none too sure).

Squid and French Bean Salad with Gari

I've always thought the most fun bit of sushi are those little flakes
of pickle sweet/hot pickled ginger, know as gari. I bought some
once with a view of treating myself to the odd titbit when no one
was looking, you know, one of those secret, hidden vice things.
Anyway, one evening I thought of using it to liven up the other
ingredients in this dish, and, by golly, it did.

250g squid
extra-virgin olive oil
400g French beans
salt
juice of ¼ lemon
50g gari

1.   Clean and slice the squid into thin strips.

2.   Heat 1tbsp olive oil in a frying pan.

3.   When it's really smoking, toss in the squid. Fry for 1 minute
     at the most, then take out and cool.

4.   Bring a pan of water (preferably low calcium) to the boil.

5. In go the French beans. On goes the lid. Cook fast for 3 to 4 minutes. They should be firm but not squeaky.

6. Drain, plunge into cold water, then drain again thoroughly.

7. Put them into a serving bowl and add the squid.

8. Dress with the salt, lemon juice and olive oil.

9. Stir in the slices of gari, making sure they are well distributed.

Spiced Roast Chicken Wings

Why do people always go for chicken breasts or even thighs and stick their noses up at chicken wings? Search me. I've usually got a few hanging about, for making stocks or for this kind of finger food, sticky and messy and rather compulsive. Just the ticket for Saturday lunch or a weekday snack.

35g ginger
juice of ½ lemon
¼ tsp turmeric
¼ tsp cumin
2 dry red chillies finely chopped
1 cup apple juice
2 tbsp olive oil
salt and pepper
8 chicken wings

1. Peel the ginger (the easiest way to peel ginger is by rubbing off the skin with a teaspoon; curious but true) and grate it.

2. Put the ginger into a bowl along with all the other ingredients except the chicken wings. Mix very thoroughly.

3. Put the chicken wings into a non-reactive dish and pour the marinade over. Leave in the fridge for at least 2 hours, preferably longer.

4. Turn on oven to 180°C/350°F/Gas 4.

5. Roast the chicken wings for about 20 minutes, spooning the marinade over them from time to time until they are well lacquered.

Grilled Gammon with Roasted Asparagus

This started off life as tongue with asparagus when I raided the fridge of some friends with whom I was staying in a fit of late-night hunger pangs. However, I think the combination works just as well with gammon, and is likely to be more widely appreciated. Incidentally, you could boil up the leftover asparagus stalks along with some new potatoes, and add the potatoes to the vegetable mix.

300g fresh asparagus
extra-virgin olive oil
2 slices of gammon
pepper

1. Turn on oven to 180°C/350°F/Gas 4.

2. Bend each asparagus over until it snaps.

3. Lay each head in a roasting tray into which you have sloshed some olive oil.

4. Dribble a little more oil on top.

5. Pop into the oven for about 15 minutes, turning the asparagus over after 7 minutes.

6. Grill the gammon slices for about 4 minutes on each side, until well tanned. Season with pepper.

7. Divide up the asparagus and put the gammon slices on top.

Chickpea and Fennel Salad

As you may have guessed, few of my dishes come about as the result of careful planning. Too often it's a matter of, 'oh-my-god, what are we going to eat? What's in the fridge/freezer/larder?' This was no exception. I had the chickpeas from a few nights previously, and I had the fennel from – well, for too long; it was going a bit brown around the edges. So I chopped it up into segments, dowsed it in a bit of this and that, and hey presto – Chickpea and Fennel Salad, mealy and crunchy, mushroomy and aniseedy and tomato-y and generally rather satisfactory, along with a little Cold Belly Pork (see Chapter 4) or even a grilled sardine or two.

150g chickpeas
1 small onion
1 stick celery
3 cloves garlic
115ml olive oil
55g tomato concentrate
500g ripe tomatoes, chopped (or 1 x 400g tin of chopped tomatoes)
1 large fennel
1 carrot
4 leaves sage
1 sprig rosemary
basil

1. Soak the chickpeas in cold water overnight. Drain.

2. Put the chickpeas into a saucepan and cover with fresh

cold water. Bring to the boil, turn down to a simmer and cook until soft.

3. Finely chop the onion, carrot, celery, and garlic.

4. Heat the olive oil in a saucepan large enough to take chickpeas and everything else. Add the onions, carrot, celery and garlic and the herbs.

5. Fry gently until the onion is soft.

6. Stir in the tomato concentrate.

7. Cut the fennel into slim segments vertically (keeping back the feathery bits for the end) and add to the chickpeas.

8. Add the tomatoes and stew over a medium heat for 20 minutes.

9. Tip in the fennel and chickpeas and stew for a further 10 minutes, but be careful not to let the florets get too soft.

10. Decant to serving dish. Cool.

11. Dot the feathery fennel bits around the cool chickpea stew.

Cavalo Nero with Garlic, Chilli and Breadcrumbs

Who had heard of cavalo nero in this country ten years ago? Suddenly those long, lancet, chewily textured leaves are everywhere, and very yummy they are too (although no more than that of our own homelier curly kale in my view). Still, they lend themselves to robust treatment, which has much to recommend it. The secret of this Italian-inspired recipe lies in the breadcrumbs. And the garlic. All right. And the cavalo nero.

250g cavalo nero
1 onion
3 cloves garlic
100ml olive oil
2tbsp breadcrumbs

1. Strip the dark-green leaf bit from the central rib, roughly chop and wash thoroughly.

2. Dry as thoroughly as you washed it.

3. Finely chop the onion and garlic.

4. Heat the olive oil in a saucepan or wok until mazy.

5. Add the onion and garlic and fry for a further 10 minutes over a gentle heat.

6. Add the cavalo nero and stir around until well coated with oil and flavourings.

7. Braise over a gentle heat until the kale is soft to the tooth – about 10 to 15 minutes should do it.

8. Fry the breadcrumbs in a little oil until brown and crunchy. Sprinkle over the cavalo nero and serve.

Leek and Pea Purée

Casting around one evening for something to go with a bit of steamed plaice, I put together this combination, and was so pleased with it, I have used it when stuck for inspiration ever since. Originally it was paired up with fishcakes (see page 68), but it goes splendidly with chicken or pork or plain fish.

2 leeks
60g butter
2 strips of lemon peel
250g frozen peas
salt and pepper

1. Slice the leeks, green tops and all.

2. Wash thoroughly to make sure there's no grit or mud lurking around.

3. Melt the butter in a pan.

4. Put the leeks into the foaming butter, add the lemon peel and a little water, perhaps 80 – 100ml, bring to a simmer, clap the lid on the pan, turn down the heat and leave to cook for about 10 minutes.

5. Add the peas and cook for a further 2 minutes.

6. Purée in a food processor. If you want it smooth, purée it a lot. If you like it rough, less so. Season to your taste.

Mashed Bananas, Strawberry Jam and Cream

Joy of my youth. Not sophisticated, not clever, not eye candy, but oh, so yummy.

3 bananas
pot of strawberry jam
1x284ml pot of the very best cream you can buy,
but not the extra thick (it's too gluey for this dish)
caster sugar (optional)

1. Peel bananas and mash.

2. Strew 1tbsp of strawberry jam all over it.

3. Pour on as much cream as you like.

4. Mash some more. Sprinkle with sugar if you have a seriously
   sweet tooth. Eat and rejoice.

✌ no sweat ✌

Coco Bean, Garlic and Parsley Soup

This soup is of the soothing and sexy variety. The bean body
of the soup is smooth, almost suave (or should be). The parsley
adds a fresh, grassy note and the garlic shavings give a touch
of panache. I prefer coco beans, which are a smaller and rounder
haricot, and have a delicate, nutty flavour. You can use ordinary
haricot blanc or cannellini beans just as well.

50g dried coco or any white beans
(or 1 can of cooked cannellini beans)
8 cloves garlic
1 medium onion
1 stick celery
1 bunch flat-leaf parsley
120ml extra-virgin olive oil
250ml chicken or vegetable stock
salt and pepper

1. If you are using dried beans, soak them overnight or all day.

2. Bring a large pot of unsalted water to the boil. Put in the
   beans and 6 garlic cloves, peeled or unpeeled as you fancy.

3. Boil until almost soft – somewhere between 1 and 1½ hours.

Drain. (If you are using tins there is no need for any of this. Just open the beans and drain them.)

4. While that is going on, finely chop the onion, celery and parsley.

5. Rinse out the saucepan and then put in half the oil.

6. Add the onion and celery and fry over a gentle heat until soft but not coloured.

7. Add the beans and stock, bring to simmering point and cook until the beans are edibly soft.

8. Take out 2tbsp of beans and a cup of water and whizz until smooth in a blender, food processor or put through a mouli. The result should be a thick cream which you will stir back into the pot with the beans.

9. Finely slice the 2 remaining garlic cloves and fry in a little oil until nut brown and crisp. Be very careful. You don't want to burn them.

10. Season and stir in the parsley.

11. When you serve it up, scatter the crisp garlic shavings over the surface and dribble – not drizzle, mind – the rest of the oil over the beans in each of the plates.

Stuffed Frittata

Frittatas are all over the place like a rash these days, but there's nothing wrong with that because they're omelettes by another name as far as I can make out. You can make them out of virtually anything – they're a very good way of using up small amounts of leftovers.

2 cloves garlic
3 courgettes
60ml olive oil
6 eggs
1 bunch parsley
2dsp grated Parmesan
2 slices ham
250g mozzarella
salt and pepper

1. Peel the cloves of garlic.

2. Slice the courgettes.
3. Heat the olive oil in a frying pan (a nonstick one will make cooking the frittata much easier).

4. Add the garlic cloves and fry until golden brown.
    Take out the garlic.

5. Add the courgettes and fry rapidly until just browned.
    Take out and keep warm.

6. Beat the eggs in a bowl.

7. Finely chop the parsley and add to the eggs and Parmesan.
    Mix thoroughly. Season with salt and pepper.

8. Pour into the frying pan and turn down the heat.

9. When the frittata is pretty much set, spread the courgette slices over the surface, then cover them with the ham slices and the mozzarella cut into bits.

10. Fold over and brush with oil.

11. Pop it under the grill until the cheese melts and the top is brown.

One evening I was tired of having a good old mustardy vinaigrette (made with peanut oil, incidentally; so much better than olive oil in this case) to help a brace of large artichokes along, so I decided to go for something with a bit more heft, and this dish was the result. Of course it's more trouble, but every now and then it's good to stretch yourself. Or indulge yourself.

2 globe artichokes
1 onion
¼ bulb fennel
½ celery stick
olive oil
3 slices prosciutto (or pancetta or bacon)
1 bunch thyme
150g fresh tomatoes (1 tin of tomatoes)
1 bunch flat-leaf parsley
salt and pepper

1. Put a large pan of water on to boil.

2. Trim the bottom of the artichokes so they can sit flat on a plate.

3. When the water is boiling, hurl them in.

4. Cook for 15 to 20 minutes.

5. Dice the onion, fennel and celery as fine as you can.

6. Heat some olive oil in a pan and add the diced veg to this when it's quite hot.

7. Cook over a medium heat until the vegetables are softish.

8. Slice the prosciutto into thin strips and add this to the veg along with the thyme.

9. Add the tomatoes and cook away until everything is quite concentrated. Season with salt and pepper.

10. When it has finished cooking, finely chop the parsley and add it along with the thyme to the mixture to infuse.

11. Open out the artichokes until you can get at the choke. Pull it out and throw away.

12. Place an artichoke on each plate and plop a ladleful of tomato/ prosciutto glop over the top, having removed the bunch of thyme. A quick splash of olive oil and down the hatch.

Grilled Plaice with Braised Romaine Lettuce, Ham and Peas

All my life I have had a weakness for petits pois a la francaise, peas cooked in white wine and stock with onions and bacon. And all my life I have had a weakness for cream. So I brought two of my (many) weaknesses together to make this vegetable stew to go with some plaice. Of course you could use most other fish just as well – salmon, cod, monkfish, sole. But not herring, mackerel, sardines or tuna.

The vegetables
1 bunch of spring onions
2 slices of ham
20g butter
200g frozen petits pois
1 heart of romaine lettuce
70ml chicken stock
lemon juice
100ml double cream
salt and pepper

1. Trim the onions.

2. Slice the ham into matchsticks.

3. Heat the butter in a saucepan. Add the onion and fry gently until soft. Add the ham, and the peas and the leaves of the romaine lettuce sliced. Pour in the chicken stock, and simmer gently for 20 minutes. Season with salt and pepper. Add a squeeze of lemon juice and the cream.

The fish
2 plaice
melted butter
salt and pepper

1. Turn on the grill.

2. Brush the fish with melted butter and season with salt and pepper.

3. Grill for 4 minutes on each side. Serve with the vegetables.

Pork Chops in Cider and Carrots

You can brine these chops first (see Grilled Pork Chops, Chapter 5), but, strictly speaking, there's no need to as you will be braising them, and that should keep them succulent. The carrots add sweetness, which seems to tango along very nicely with that of the cider.

300g carrots
2tbsp peanut oil
110g unsalted butter
2 pork chops
salt and pepper
200ml sweet cider
100ml chicken stock
2 sprigs thyme

1. Peel and slice the carrots thinly.

2. Heat the oil and butter in a sauté pan or a deep frying pan until smoking. Quickly brown the pork chops on both sides. Take out.

3. Add the carrots.

4. Lay the pork chops on top of the vegetables. Season.

5. Add the cider, turn up the heat and boil the cider to reduce by half.

6. Add the stock, turn the heat down again and cook gently for 15 to 20 minutes.

7. Taste the sauce. If it doesn't seem intense enough to you, pour it off and boil it down until it does.

8. Sprinkle the leaves from the thyme sprigs just before serving.

Golden Fried Potatoes with Bacon and Sausages

Holiday food, weekend food, weekday food, easy food, easy-to-love food. I ate it first on a yacht bobbing among the Greek islands, believe it or not. It seemed pretty fabulous to me then, and it still does. All right, have a green salad on the side, if you must. And a bottle of rosé, I fancy.

6 chipolata sausages (or Italian luganica or Greek sausages)
150g pancetta or unsmoked bacon cut as thinly as possible
500g potatoes
500ml olive oil
salt and pepper

1. Cut the sausages into 5cm lengths. Grill or fry until brown and crunchy. Grill or fry the bacon until crisp. The crisp bit is very important.

2. Cut the potatoes into small chips – French-fry size.

3. Bring the oil to smoking temperature in a large pan. Throw in the chips and fry until golden and crisp. You may have to do this in batches.

4. Scoop them out when done and dry on kitchen towel.

5. Mix in the bacon and sausage and pile them all onto a large warm plate. Season and serve.

Couscous-stuffed Courgettes with Harissa and Tomato Sauce

Courgettes usually get a supporting roll when it comes to firing up the dishes. And then one summer, I started having a glut of them. Courgette piled on courgette, although technically speaking I suppose they were zucchini as they were a variety called Romanesco, heavily ridged and very tasty. In a desperate attempt to persuade my family to eat just one more helping, in a bold move I decided to move them from crowd scene to centre stage with this sort of Moroccan-effect dish.

4 medium courgettes
50g couscous
55g raisins
1 onion
olive oil
15g pine kernels
½ tsp cumin
Mint (enough to make 1 tbsp when chopped)
½ tsp allspice
salt and pepper

1. Turn on the oven to 180°C/350°F/Gas 4.

2. Slice the courgettes in half lengthways.

3. Scoop out the seeds with a spoon and put to one side, leaving a trench the length of each half-courgette.

4. Blanch in a pot of salted water for 3 to 4 minutes until half-cooked.

5. Drain and dry on kitchen towel.

6. Put the couscous and raisins in a bowl, cover with boiling water and leave to steep for 10 minutes.

7. Chop up the onion finely.

8. Fry in olive oil until translucent. Take out and add to the couscous.

9. Fry the pine kernels in the same oil until they begin to brown and add to the rest.

10. Fry the cumin seeds until they begin to pop and add them along with the all spice, raisins, their water and the mint cut into strips.

11. Mix all the stuffing ingredients in a bowl. Season well.

12. Arrange the courgette halves on an oiled baking tray, hollow side up.

13. Heap the stuffing into each until it is all gone. It doesn't matter if some of it falls off.

14. Cover with foil, put in the oven and bake for 20 minutes. Serve with the sauce below.

Harissa and Tomato Sauce

150g very ripe tomatoes
3tbsp olive oil
pinch of sugar
1tsp harissa
pinch of salt

1. Plunge the tomatoes into boiling water for 30 seconds. Take out and peel. (You can omit this stage if you are really lazy.)

2. Cut the tomatoes in half and scoop out the seeds. (You can omit this stage if you are really pushed for time.)

3. Put the tomatoes, sugar, salt and olive oil in a blender or food processor and whizz until liquid.

4. Pass through a sieve if you want a completely smooth sauce.

5. Stir in the harissa and season to taste. It is designed to be served cold, but of course you can warm it if you wish.

Crusted Cauliflower

I love the creamy, white head of a fresh cauli, like a ball made from sea foam. They may not have the glamour of an artichoke, say, or even broccoli, but, damn it, they are lovely when treated with understanding, quite able to take their place among the pantheon of great vegetables.

1 small head cauliflower
2 cloves garlic
1tbsp stoned black olives
1 bunch flat-leaf parsley
2tbsp breadcrumbs
2tbsp olive oil

salt and pepper

1. Turn on the oven to 180°C/350°F/Gas 4.

2. Trim all the leaves off the cauliflower. Break the head up
    into chunks.

3. Bring a pan of water to the boil.

4. Plunge the cauli florets in, and cook for 5 to 10 minutes until
    they are just cooked through.

5. Drain thoroughly and spread them out in a baking dish.

6. Chop the garlic finely. Chop the olives and parsley not quite
    so finely. Put all these into a bowl, along with the
    breadcrumbs and olive oil. Season with salt and pepper.

7. Mix thoroughly and spoon over the cauli bits.

8. Slide into the oven and bake until the topping has gone
    crunchy, about 15 minutes.

Roasted Peaches on Parkin

I like to think that not everyone would think of this particular
combination. There's something about the sweet acidity of the
peaches and the light heat of the ginger in the parkin that, well,
I don't know, just hits the spot.

4 slices of parkin (or other ginger bread)
2 medium ripe peaches
unsalted butter
demerara sugar

1. Turn on the oven to 180°C/350°F/Gas 4.

2. Butter one side of the parkin slices generously.

3. Arrange in a roasting tray, buttered-side down.

4. Cut the peaches in half and lay cut-side down on the parkin slice. Dot with unsalted butter and sprinkle with demerara sugar.

5. Pop into the oven for 5 to 10 minutes, until the bottom of the parkin slices has gone all crisp. Serve immediately. (With double cream, if you like.)

❧ making an effort ❧

Beetroot, Feta and Rocket Terrine

Desperate times call for desperate measures. A friend announced that he was dropping in somewhat unexpectedly and I had to rustle up lunch in pretty short order. As he was a food writer of some eminence, I couldn't exactly do baked beans on toast. This was the first course.

1 or 2 beetroot, depending on size
1 handful rocket
25g grated Parmesan
juice of ¼ lemon
extra-virgin olive oil
150g feta cheese

1. Boil or roast the beetroot until cooked through. Peel and cool.

2. Blitz the rocket, Parmesan and lemon juice with just enough

olive oil to keep it squidgy, but not liquid.

3. Line 4 ramekins with clingfilm. The edges of the clingfilm should extend well over the edge of the ramekins.

4. Put a thickish slice of beetroot on the base of the ramekin.

5. Crumble the feta cheese and put down a layer about 1cm thick on top of the beetroot.

6. Spread the rocket and Parmesan sludge on the feta in a good layer. Repeat the process until the ramekin is full.

7. Fold the clingfilm over the top and press down firmly to compact the layers.

8. Put into the fridge to chill until needed.

9. When you need them, turn them out onto a plate and peel off the clingfilm. With a bit of luck you won't even have to wash the ramekins.

10. Dribble a little olive oil over them, or even lemon-flavoured oil if you have it. Good bread would be nice, too.

Gnocchi di Ricotta et Spinaci

My brother Johnny, who lives in Rome, made this for me after one of those hideous journeys that seem to be part and parcel of modern air travel. It restored my faith in humanity.

350g ricotta
150g frozen spinach thawed
or fresh spinach weighed when cooked
50g grated Parmesan

2 whole eggs
nutmeg
salt and pepper
200g plain flour

1. Place the ricotta into a large bowl and beat it until smoothish.

2. Dry the spinach well and chop finely.

3. Add the spinach and the Parmesan to the ricotta.

4. Add one of the eggs and mix well. If the consistency is dry, add all or part of the second egg but do not get the mixture too wet or it will be difficult to handle.

5. Season with grated nutmeg to taste (the flavour is lost a little in the cooking and so you should add a bit more than you think is necessary), salt and a good grinding of black pepper.

6. Cover the mixture and pop into the fridge for at least an hour.

7. When you want to form the gnocchi, cover a large plate or tray with a good centimetre of flour.

8. Drop a dessertspoonful of the gnocchi mixture, gently roll it until you can pick it up in floured hands, and roll them into flour-covered balls.

9. Put these onto the generously floured second tray.

10. Drop the gnocchi into a large, wide pan of gently simmering water, 6 or 7 at a time.

11. Wait until they float to the surface, let them cook for

a further 30 seconds and then scoop them out gently with a slotted spoon.

12. Drain well.

13. Put them into an ovenproof dish with a little tomato sauce on the bottom of the dish, and pour a little more sauce over them.

14. Keep the cooked ones warm while you're poaching the rest of the gnocchi.

15. When all the gnocchi are cooked, cover generously with tomato sauce (see Johnny's Souped-up Salsa di Pomodoro, Chapter 7) and serve the grated Parmesan cheese separately. The gnocchi should be translucent and light.

Lentils with Poached Egg

I love this recipe. It's the way the egg yolk sinks down into the lentils when you cut into it, lubricating them and giving them a soothingly unctuous smoothness. Very indulgent. And healthy, too. Cook loads of lentils. They freeze well and are a very good stand-by.

1 carrot
1 onion
1 stick celery
1 leek
2 rashers of smoked bacon
115ml olive oil
125g Puy, Casteluccio or similar small slate-green lentils
(red and brown ones will not do)
350ml stock (chicken or vegetable)
1tsp nam pla (Vietnamese fish sauce) – optional

1 dsp red-wine vinegar – optional
1 tsp Dijon mustard – optional
salt and pepper
2 eggs

1. Finely chop the vegetables and the bacon. To be truthful,
   I do the carrot, celery and leek in the food processor.
   Heresy, I know, but there you are, I'm a lazy cook. But
   I always chop the onion by hand. Onions do not take
   kindly to processing.

2. Heat the olive oil in a saucepan and, when mazy with heat,
   add the vegetables, stirring to coat them in oil.

3. Cook over a medium heat for 5 to 7 minutes, stirring
   occasionally, until they are well wilted, the onion is
   transparent and fat is running from the bacon.

4. Rinse the lentils under cold water and add them to the
   vegetables, stirring them around.

5. Add the stock, bring to the boil and simmer until the lentils
   are tender but have not disintegrated. This could take
   anywhere between 15 to 25 minutes, depending on your
   lentils. You just have to try them from time to time. Cool
   slightly and add the flavourings of your choice.

I serve these by putting a tablespoon or two into a ramekin,
plonking the poached egg on top and then eat it with a teaspoon.
But there's no need to be so refined. On the plate with the egg
on top is just fine. I am not going to tell you how to poach an
egg. A fried egg is almost as good, but not quite.

Duck Breasts with Figs and Fig Balsamic Vinegar

4 duck breasts
8 bay leaves
4tbsp fig (or apple, or straight) balsamic vinegar
8 figs
salt and pepper

1. Turn on the oven to 150°C/300°F/Gas 2.

2. Carefully peel the skin back off the duck breasts, but still leaving it just attached at one end.

3. Place two bay leaves on each breast and cover with the skin. Season with salt and pepper.

4. Place on a roasting tray, skin-side down.

5. Pour balsamic vinegar over each breast.

6. Roast for 1 hour, basting from time to time.

7. Pop under the grill to crisp up the skin if not crisp enough already.

8. Chop up the figs roughly or slice them and heap onto each plate.

9. Serve the breasts, dividing the juices between breasts and figs.

I was on my way back from the station when I got the call.
Supper. What was I going to do about supper? Oh. Er, er.
Make a quick detour to a supermarket that shall remain
nameless to search for inspiration. This recipe was the result.

400g haddock
salt and pepper
200g potatoes, floury ones such as Golden Wonder, King Edward,
Pentland Crown, Cara
large bunch of broad-leaf parsley
75g hot spicy sausage (e.g. chorizo)
2 eggs
matzo meal or breadcrumbs
2tbsp of olive oil
55g butter

1. Turn on the oven to 180°C/350°F/Gas 4.

2. Wrap the fish in foil, having seasoned it lightly with salt
   and pepper.

3. Pop it in the oven and bake for 10 minutes. If you have
   any fish already cooked, so much the better.

4. Boil the potatoes until cooked through.

5. Remove from the water and peel as soon as you can.

6. Put into a bowl and mash with a fork or masher.

7. Add the fish, and break up with the fork, but not too much.
   I like chunky bits of fish in my cakes.

8. Chop the parsley and the chorizo. You want nuggets of
   chorizo, not paste.

9. Add to the fish/potato combo along with 1 egg, and mix well.

10. Form into fishcakes as thick and as large as you like.

11. Take the other egg and beat well. Pour it onto a plate.

12. Pour a couple of tablespoons of matzo meal or breadcrumbs onto a second plate.

13. When you are ready to cook the fishcakes, heat the butter and oil in a frying pan.

14. Dip the fishcakes first in the egg, then in the meal/ breadcrumbs, taking care that they don't fall apart, and then slip them gently into the foaming fat.

15. Fry until crisp and brown on either side.

16. Alternatively, you needn't bother with any of that palaver. Just grill them for 3 to 4 minutes on either side until they are tanned and golden. I think you could probably just roast them in a high oven (220°C/425°F/Gas 7) but I haven't tried it.

Smoked Haddock and Chard in Mustard Custard

This is a superior offering, fit for a dinner party as well as a supper for two (with some cheese and fruit to come after.) Anyway, I just love those smoky, meaty collops of cured haddock.

200g undyed smoked haddock
250ml full-cream milk
200g chard (green part only)
2 whole eggs
1dsp whole-grain mustard
salt

1. Turn on the oven to 180°C/350°F/Gas 4.

2. Divide the haddock into 4 pieces. Put the haddock in a dish and pour the milk over. Pop into the oven and poach for 20 minutes. Take the haddock out of the milk, cover and keep warm.

3. Wash the chard, strip out the white stems and shake off as much water as possible. Cook in the microwave for 1 minute (the chard keeps its vibrant dark-green colour and you won't have to squeeze the spinach to get rid of the water, so the leaves keep their shape).

4. Beat the eggs and half the milk in which you have cooked the haddock together, then beat in the mustard and season if necessary. Stir in the chard.

5. Decant the mixture into a buttered dish or soufflé mould, or even two ramekins.

6. Put into a roasting or baking dish, fill halfway up with boiling water and pop into the oven. Bake for 30 minutes until the custard has set.

7. Serve with the haddock (or you could flake the haddock and mix it in with the other ingredients as part of stage 4).

Griddled Chicken Breast, Aubergine and Chillied Tomato

Simple, light, quick, delicious – what more do you want? Please don't say healthy. OK, yes, it is that, too. And of course you can grill or even fry the chicken breast and aubergine in olive oil if you don't have a griddle. You just won't get those pretty black scorch marks, that's all.

1 aubergine
extra-virgin olive oil
200g tomatoes
2 shallots
1 dried birdseye chilli
fresh basil leaves
2 chicken breasts
salt and pepper

1. Turn on the oven 180°C/350°F/Gas 4.

2. Slice the aubergine in half and take a thin slice off the curved outside as well so they will lie flat on a baking tray.

3. Splash with olive oil and put into the oven for 30 to 40 minutes.

4. Chop the tomatoes up roughly.

5. Chop up the shallots and the chilli and scatter all over. Splash olive oil over them and bung them in the oven along with the aubergines for the same time.

6. Tip the tomatoes, shallots and chilli into a bowl and mash up with a fork.

7. Tear up a few basil leaves and stir in.

8. Heat the griddle pan until smoking. Lay the chicken breasts on it and leave for 6 minutes. Turn over and leave for another 6 minutes. Season with salt and pepper.

9. Take off the heat and move to a heated oven to rest for 5 minutes or so.

10. Spread half the tomato pulp on one aubergine half and half on the other.

11. Put the griddled chicken breast on top. Splash a little olive oil around for scenic effect. A salad on the side, perhaps?

Broccoli with Garlic

Frankly, a man can get bored with broccoli, the great stand-by vegetable. Occasionally it needs a little help. I won't make any great claims for originality for this recipe, but it does give the old broccoli a bit of a lift. Add some finely chopped chilli, if you fancy. The Calabrians would. Or chopped anchovy fillets.

1 head of broccoli (Romanesco if you can find it)
2 cloves of garlic
3tbsp olive oil
Juice of ½ lemon
salt and pepper

1. Break up the heads of broccoli into florets.

2. Peel and slice the garlic finely.

3. Put the broccoli into a pan with the olive oil, lemon juice and about 115ml water. Bring to the boil and continue boiling rapidly until the water has evaporated, leaving the broccoli glossy with olive oil and lemon juice. You will need to turn them from time to time, but carefully because you don't want a mush.

4. When the liquid is gone, season the broccoli and keep it warm.

5. Fry the garlic slivers until they are light brown and crisp, and sprinkle over the top of the broccoli when you serve it.

The marriage of rhubarb and strawberries was revealed to me by the great Georges Blanc of Vonnas, or, to be absolutely honest, his book, Cuisine Naturelle. The two different acidities and flavours work off each other beautifully. He does his a bit differently.

375g butter puff pastry
500g rhubarb
2tbsp honey
250g strawberries
butter

1. Turn on the oven to 180°C/350°F/Gas 4.

2. Butter a flan dish.

3. Roll out the pastry so it will fit inside the dish and place it inside the dish.

4. Place the rhubarb stalks uncut on top in a line.

5. Dribble the honey over all. Dot with butter.

6. Slip it into the oven for 30 to 35 minutes until the pastry is golden brown and the rhubarb quite soft. Cool.

7. Hull and slice the strawberries vertically into 4.

8. Arrange the strawberry slices decoratively on top. Sprinkle with a little sugar.

4. four all

I won't say that cooking for four people is twenty times more
fun than cooking for two, but we're definitely stepping up a gear.
I mean, you might be cooking for just the family, casually, on
a Friday night, or something. Or it could be friends round,
and when friends are round, things tend to become a bit more
competitive, a bit more showy offy, so you need to be prepared.
Still, we're not at the stage or the outright warfare that dinner
parties for six or eight bring on. Cooking for four still suggests
a fairly relaxed and informal process to me, like a Saturday lunch
or something easy-going during the week. Of course, I've tried
to cover the options just to make sure you aren't caught out by
a sudden shift in the social winds.

❧ a piece of cake ❧

Aubergine and Ricotta Spread

The first time I had this in Sicily, it was made with pecorino, which brought a sharp, salty tang to the mix. You could try that if you want and can get hold of a good version. Parmesan works well, too, but I prefer ricotta because its gentle creaminess seems to fold into the smoky smoothness of the aubergine so cosily.

250g aubergine
100g pecorino cheese
juice of ½ lemon
extra-virgin olive oil (optional)
salt and pepper

1. Grill the aubergines until the flesh is soft and the skin charred.

2. Holding them by the stalk, peel and then leave in a colander for 30 minutes or so to drain. Mash up with a fork.

3. Grate the pecorino and stir into the aubergine glop.

4. Add the lemon juice, perhaps a little olive oil, then salt and pepper.

Courgette, Thyme, Lemon and Garlic Spread

200g courgettes
2 cloves garlic
extra-virgin olive oil infused with lemon
juice of ½ lemon
2 sprigs thyme
salt and pepper

1. Wash and slice the courgettes.

2. Crush the garlic.

3. Heat 2tbsp lemon-infused olive oil in a frying pan. Add the garlic and fry gently until it begins to colour.

4. Add the lemon juice and a little water, maybe 2-3tbsp. Cook gently until the courgettes are very soft. Pull off the thyme leaves and scatter over. Mash thoroughly and season.

Spaghetti Frittata

When my daughter, Lois, was growing up, she would have been quite happy eating pasta for breakfast, lunch and dinner. I always tried to make a bit more than even she could eat so that we'd have a bit left over which I could turn into frittata. This is the basic version. I have added anchovies and capers in my time (not a huge success with Lois), bacon, ham, layers of tomato and courgettes and mozzarella (which went down a storm).

1 bunch parsley
2tbsp grated Parmesan
8 eggs
250g cooked spaghetti
olive oil
salt and pepper

1. Chop the parsley finely and grate the Parmesan.

2. Beat the eggs in a bowl. Season with pepper.

3. Pour the spaghetti into the bowl with the eggs and mix thoroughly.

4. Stir in the parsley. Mix thoroughly again.

5. Add the grated Parmesan. Mix again.

6. Heat the oil in a nonstick frying pan. When smoking, pour the egg and spaghetti mixture in. Fry gently until the top is just set. The correct procedure at this point is to slide it out onto a plate, and then plonk it back, top down, back in the pan to continue cooking for a few more minutes. But if, like me, you are not up for that daredevil stuff, pop it under the grill or into the oven (170°C/325°F/Gas 3) for 5-10 minutes or so until firm. Eat hot.

Broad Bean and Potato Soup with Chorizo

I hardly ever order a soup in a restaurant. At home it's another matter. Soup seems to hit the spot much more often. And let's face it, they're not hard to make. This one was another consequence of an ongoing oh-not-broad-beans-again situation. They were getting a bit coarse and mealy, too, by this time, which made them a harder sell. However, with a few chunks of chorizo to cheer it on, the soup slipped down without a murmur of complaint.

1kg fresh broad beans
1 litre chicken or vegetable stock
400g potatoes
200g chorizo
salt and pepper

1. Pod the beans.

2. Bring the stock to boiling point. Add the beans and simmer until soft – about 10 minutes. Whizz up in a food processor and then pass through a mouli on a medium sieve.

3. Peel the potatoes and cut into dice-sized squares. Slice the

chorizo into thin rounds or squares or whatever shape will fit easily on a spoon. Reheat the soup.

4. Add the potatoes and chorizo. Simmer gently until the potato is cooked.

5. Season and serve.

For a vegetarian variation, use vegetable stock, drop the chorizo and swirl in a teaspoon or so of harissa.

Grilled Guinea Fowl with Chilli and Lemon

The guinea fowl lies somewhere between a chicken and a pheasant in my book. They do have rather more flavour than all but the very finest chickens, and sometimes more than pheasants, too, to which they are closer in size. The thing is they take this Southern Italian treatment very well. A useful dish to have in the repertoire as it is as easy to make as it is delicious to eat.

2 guinea fowl, preferably free range
1 peperoncino or birdseye chilli
salt and pepper
2 cloves garlic
3 organic or unwaxed lemons
olive oil
1 large bunch parsley

1. Spatchcock the guinea fowl by cutting through the backbone and flattening the birds out.

2. Chop up the chilli finely, and mix with salt and pepper.

3. Crush the garlic lightly.

4. Lay the guinea fowl skin-side down on the grill tray.

Sprinkle a little olive oil over them.

5. Cut the lemons into quarters. Squeeze the juice over the birds, taking care to get rid of the pips. Place the pieces of lemon peel over the surface of the fowl to protect it from getting too burned too soon.

6. Grill for 25 minutes, basting with olive oil and lemon juice.

7. Turn over. Sprinkle the salt/pepper/chilli mixture over them. Grill for another 15 minutes or until they are nicely tanned. Baste from time to time.

8. Chop the parsley and scatter liberally over all.

9. Rest for 10 minutes before serving up with plenty of the oily, lemony juices over the meat.

Zucchini with Chilli, Garlic and Mint

As long as you don't mind a bit of chilli in your life, this dish goes very well with the guinea fowl above. All in all, it's very refreshing, too. Good for a warm summer's day.

125ml red-wine vinegar
3 cloves garlic
2 dried red chillies
8 zucchini
150ml olive oil
salt and pepper
handful of mint

1. Pour the vinegar in a serving bowl. Crush the garlic and add to the vinegar.

2. Cut up the chillies. Cut the zucchini into sticks about
    1 cm thick.

3. Heat the olive oil in a frying pan. Throw in the zucchini
    and the chilli and fry rapidly until golden, about 4 minutes,
    turning frequently.

4. Turn the zucchini onto some kitchen towel.

5. Season and then transfer while still hot to the vinegar,
    turning them in it so they have been thoroughly coated.

6. Chop up the mint quite roughly and scatter over the zucchini.

Butternut Squash and Gruyere Mash

This, on the other hand, is a rich and soothing number to
keep out the cool chills of autumn. Fine with any roasted
or grilled meats.

600g butternut squash flesh
(approx 750g butternut squash, skin and seeds included)
40g butter
salt and pepper
250g Gruyere
2tbsp breadcrumbs

1. Turn the oven on to 180°C/350°F/Gas 4.

2. Cut up the squash, scrape out the seeds and roast for
    25 minutes until easily pierced with a knife. Carve off
    the pumpkin flesh and transfer to a bowl.

3. Add the butter and season well.

4. Grate the Gruyere. Add 150g of the grated cheese to the squash, and beat in thoroughly to make sure it is properly distributed.

5. Scrape the mixture into a baking dish. Scatter the breadcrumbs and the rest of the cheese on top.

6. Put the dish into the oven and cook until the top has melted and gone brown and crunchy. If this seems to be taking too long, pop it under the grill until it has.

Honey-braised Quinces on Brioche

Sometimes I think if you braised an old telephone book with quinces, it would turn out wonderfully edible. Quinces are one of the great transforming ingredients (hollandaise sauce and fat are others), adding their perfumed, amber lustre to lamb or duck, say, or pears. But then they are utterly wonderful on their own.

8 quinces
1tbsp clear honey
25g unsalted butter
4 slices of brioche
a bit more butter
caster or icing sugar

1. Turn on the oven to 180°C/350°F/Gas 4.

2. Peel, core and slice the quinces into whatever shapes you fancy.

3. Heat the honey and butter in a pan with a little water.

4. Add the quince slices. Braise for 7 or 8 minutes until the quince is easily pierced with the end of a knife.

5. Butter each slice of brioche on both sides and arrange on a baking tray. Bake for 8 to 10 minutes, until the brioche looks slightly toasted.

6. Pop a brioche slice on each plate. Pile the quince slices on and serve immediately, hot or warm.

Rhubarb with Ginger and Vanilla

You might find this hard to believe, but technically speaking, rhubarb is a vegetable. But in a landmark judgement by the US Customs Court in Buffalo in 1947, it was classified as a fruit. Common sense, really, because that's how we use it. Frankly, I don't care what it is. The splendour of the rhubarb lies in the fact that it's the first fruit (or vegetable) off the blocks after winter. Ginger rubs along very nicely with it, bringing a cheery warmth to its sharp acidity. Also, a nip of ginger wine while you're cooking can give a lift to the cook's spirits and energy levels.

1kg rhubarb
50g fresh ginger
1 vanilla pod
115ml ginger wine (Crabbie's or Stones)
150g caster sugar

1. Preheat the oven to 170°C/325°F/Gas 3.

2. Cut the rhubarb into 5cm lengths.

3. Peel the ginger and slice thinly.

4. Cut the vanilla pod down the middle and put into a non-reactive dish.

5. Add the slices of ginger, the rhubarb and the ginger wine.

6. Cover tightly with foil and bake for 20 minutes.

7. Serve warm with the cooking juices poured over them, and vanilla ice cream or just plain cream.

❧ no sweat ❧

Roasted Red Pepper with Spring Onions and Anchovies

I came home late one Saturday evening feeling just a touch peckish, but didn't want a major palaver. I looked in the fridge and found, yes, a red pepper and a few old spring onions. And I always, always, have anchovy fillets somewhere. Blimey, I thought, when I finished mopping up the juices, that was nice. Pity there was no one else around to appreciate my ingenuity. Hopefully now there will be.

4 large red peppers
extra-virgin olive oil
8 anchovy fillets
16 spring onions

1. Turn on the oven to 180°C/350°F/Gas 4.

2. Cut the peppers in half and cut out all the seeds.

3. Lay those cut peppers down in a roasting tray well smeared with olive oil.

4. Put an anchovy fillet over each half-pepper.

5. Trim the spring onions to the right length and lay two in each of the pepper halves.

6. Splash some more oil over them, slide into the oven and roast for 1 hour. Eat warm or cold.

Quail with Barley and Sweet Corn Risotto

There's a story of hubris attached to this. For years I kept coming across 'risottos' in British restaurants made with barley, and each time I would fulminate against these, saying there was no such thing as a barley risotto. It was on a par with parsley 'pesto' in my book. And then I was taken to a superb restaurant in a valley northeast of Turin, which was dedicated to serving the food of the surrounding Waldensian communities. And blow me, there was a barley risotto on the menu, and very wonderful it was too. So I ate humble pie and the risotto.

140g barley (35g per person)
2 litres of chicken stock
4 quails
30g butter
115g pancetta
125g frozen sweet corn (or the corn from 2 cobs)
1 bunch thyme
salt and pepper

1. Put the barley and stock in a saucepan, bring to the boil and simmer gently until the barley is cooked – about 40 minutes.

2. Turn on the oven to 180°C/350°F/Gas 4.

3. Smear the quail with butter, season and roast for 20 minutes. Allow to rest.

4. Boil the sweet corn for 15 to 20 minutes if using fresh. Cut the corn off the cob.

5. Add the sweet corn to the barley and heat through.

6. Chop up the pancetta into whatever shapes you feel like that day and fry until crisp. Add their bits and their fat to the barley and sweet corn.

7. Stick a bunch of thyme into the barley and sweet corn mix and leave to infuse for 10 minutes.

8. Serve the quail with a helping of the mixture.

Red Mullet and Fennel Sandwich

It's a looker, this dish. Or it's supposed to be (which isn't the same as saying it's a bother to make; it isn't). And it works because that mellow, sweet aniseed of the fennel is a delicious mattress on which the peppy, distinctively favoured red mullet lies back with distinction.

2 large bulbs of fennel
olive oil
½ lemon
8 red mullet fillets
salt and pepper

1. Turn on the oven to 170°C/325°F/Gas 3.

2. Slice the fennel. You need 4 slices about 1.5-2cm thick that will hold together.

3. Splash some olive oil onto a baking tray and lay the fennel slices on it. Splash a little more olive oil on them. Sprinkle with salt. Pop into the oven for about 30 to 40 minutes, until they are soft and golden. Of course, you can get the same effect by gently frying them. When they are ready, transfer the slices to a plate or dish that you can keep warm.

4. Peel the lemon right down to the flesh. There must be no pith left. Slice the lemon across in very thin slices. You need 4 slices in all.

5. A quarter of an hour before serving, turn the oven up to maximum heat (240°C/475°F/Gas 9 or thereabouts) for 5 minutes.

6. Lay the fillets in the oil on the tray in which the fennel has been cooked. Sprinkle with a little salt and slide the tray into the oven for 5 to 7 minutes, until the fillets are cooked.

7. On each warm plate lay down one fillet. Place a slice of cooked fennel on each fillet. Cover with a slice of lemon and put the second fillet on top. Dribble a little olive oil over each and serve.

Sardines and Zucchini with Caper, Lemon and Celery Sauce

This is a summery, celebratory dish. I like the combination of raw zucchini and cooked fish because the fish is quite soft and the zucchini quite crunchy and the sauce quite right.

4 fresh sardines
4 to 6 courgettes
olive oil

1. Slit the sardines the full length of their bodies along the belly.

2. Cut off the heads and clean out the guts from the inside.

3. Take out the backbone by placing them belly down on a chopping board and pressing down hard. The sides of the fish should spread out on either side, causing the side bones to spring away from the flesh. It should be quite an easy matter

now to get a fingernail under the backbone and ease it away
from the flesh, leaving you with, effectively, 2 fillets of fish
joined by a flap of skin at the top. Cut down the flap so the
2 fillets are separate.

4. Alternatively you can fillet them in the conventional way,
   or, best of all, get your fishmonger to fillet them for you.

5. Slice the courgettes lengthways into strips about 5mm thick
   or less.

6. Heat 55ml of the oil in a nonstick frying pan until smoking.

7. Fry the sardine fillets for 1 to 1½ minutes on either side
   (or for 3 minutes on one side if they are too fragile to
   turn over).

8. Place one of the sardine fillets on a plate. Place a strip of
   courgette on top covering it. Place a fillet of sardine on top
   and then a second piece of courgette on top of that. (Or just
   make two courgette and sardine sandwiches and arrange
   beautifully on the plate.)

The sauce
2tbsp capers in vinegar or salt
leaves from 1 head of celery
juice of 1 lemon plus the peel of ½ a lemon
115ml extra-virgin olive oil

1. Place all the ingredients in a blender and whizz until smooth
   and homogenised. Alternatively, blast with a blitzer.

Chicken Thighs with Sorrel and Shallots

Like rhubarb, sorrel has a special place in the hearts of gardeners (of this one, anyway) because it pops up almost immediately after winter has decided to pack it in. And it comes back year after year without any bother. The only serious drawback with sorrel is keeping pace with its endless productivity. In the end you can't.

3 shallots
30g butter
8 chicken thighs
75ml vermouth or white wine
2 large handfuls of sorrel leaves
2tbsp crème fraîche
100ml chicken or vegetable stock
salt and pepper

1. Peel and chop the shallots finely and slice the sorrel leaves into strips.

2. Heat the butter in a deep frying pan to foaming.

3. Put in the chicken thighs. Brown on one side and then the other. Remove from the pan and keep warm.

4. If the butter is burned, pour out, wipe the pan clean with kitchen towel and melt another 30g butter. Toss in the chopped shallots and fry gently until translucent.

5. Pour in the vermouth/ white wine and boil furiously until reduced to a couple of tablespoonfuls.

6. Toss in the sorrel leaves and add the crème fraîche.

7. Put the chicken thighs back in the pan and pour the stock over them. Poach gently for 10 minutes.

Cold Belly Pork

My mother and I have been comparing notes on belly pork
for decades. This is the outcome of shared wisdom and experience,
although I think she still looks on mirin with a touch of suspicion.
But, like her, I always find it very useful to have a slab around in
case of emergencies, like a lunch or supper or a sudden attack of
nervous flutters in the tummy in between. Incidentally, try it with
a dill pickle instead of chutney (or your own pickled cucumbers if
you're really self-sufficient).

3 cloves garlic
100ml mirin
100ml rice-wine vinegar
25ml saba or cheap balsamic vinegar
1kg belly pork in one piece
water
salt and pepper

1. Turn on the oven to its lowest setting, preferably S for slow,
    i.e. about 80°C or so (no higher than 100°C).

2. Slice the garlic and scatter over the base of a roasting pan
    not much larger than the belly pork if possible.

3. Pour the other liquid ingredients except the water over
    the garlic.

4. Place the belly pork on top of these. Add the water until
    the liquids come about halfway up the meat.

5. Put into the middle of the oven and leave overnight or all
    day; definitely for 6 hours minimum. The idea is that the
    fat is slowly leached out of the meat, keeping it moist while
    it is cooking.

6. When you deem the meat to be cooked, take the belly out
    of the oven. Cool.

7. Carefully cut the skin – crackling to be – off the top. Put into another roasting pan and sprinkle with salt and pepper. Turn up the oven to 190°C/375°F/Gas 5. Pop the crackling back into the oven to crackle – about 15 to 20 minutes. Check from time to time to make sure it's not burning.

Caponata

The great Sicilian sweet and sour vegetable stew. The recipe here is a bit arbitrary, in that there are as many recipes for caponata as there are cooks in Sicily. I have known them without celery, sultanas, pine nuts, olives and capers. I have eaten them with almonds, octopus and even chocolate. The only elements that are absolutely essential are aubergines and the sweet and sour combination of sugar and vinegar.

2 black aubergines or, better still, 1 large violet one
2 sticks celery
1 medium onion
2 cloves garlic
125ml olive oil
2tsp sugar
70ml red-wine vinegar
300g tomato pulp
100g green olives
1tbsp salted capers
1tbsp sultanas
1½ tbsp pine nuts
fresh basil leaves
salt and pepper

1. Wash the aubergines and cut into cubes about 2cm square.

2. Slice the celery, onion and garlic quite finely.

3. Heat the oil in a deep frying pan or sauté pan until smoking.

4. Toss in the aubergine cubes and rapidly brown all over.

5. Add the sliced celery, onion and garlic and fry for a further couple of minutes, but gently.

6. Sprinkle the sugar over the aubergine cubes, and toss them so that they all get a bit of the sugary action. Turn the heat right down.

7. Pour in the red-wine vinegar and boil until it has disappeared.

8. Add the tomato pulp and let the aubergine stew for 15 minutes or so, until the cubes are quite soft. Season.

9. Add the olives, capers and sultanas.

10. Heat the pine nuts in a frying pan until they begin to go brown. Scatter over the aubergine.

11. Let everything cool down and get on politely exchanging flavours.

12. Tear up the basil leaves and add.

Spinach with Anchovy

Rather like the broccoli with garlic, adding anchovies is a way of jollying up a vegetable you know is good for you, but of which you're growing just a bit tired. It's rather good cold, too.

1kg spinach
1 clove garlic
4 anchovy fillets
olive oil

salt and pepper
lemon juice

1. Wash the spinach thoroughly, and then strip the green leaves from the stalks.

2. Just move the leaves to a colander. You need some of the water clinging to the leaves.

3. Peel and lightly crush the garlic. In a frying pan, wok or even wide-bottomed saucepan heat the oil, the garlic and the anchovy chopped up.

4. When the garlic is fizzing, but only golden, add the spinach leaves, and stir round to coat with oil.

5. Keep turning them over a high heat until well wilted and the water has boiled off. Take out the garlic cloves unless you really like eating them. Season with salt and pepper.

6. Squeeze a little lemon juice over the spinach when ready to eat.

Rhubarb and Brioche Sandwiches

There are plenty of recipes for rhubarb because it cheers up a time of year when there's no other seasonal fresh stuff about. Star anise adds a whiff of orientalism to the homely rhubarb.

1kg rhubarb
250g caster sugar
1 star anise
juice of 1 orange

1. Cut the rhubarb into sticks about 5-6cm long and about 1cm thick.

2. Place in a saucepan along with the sugar, star anise (make sure the star anise is well embedded among the rhubarb bits) and orange juice.

3. Clap the top on the pan, and bring to a gentle simmer.

4. Cook until the rhubarb is soft but still retains its shape. You have to be quite clever and attentive about this.

5. Leave to cool. Strain off the juices and keep to one side for making ice cream (see below).

For the Brioche
8 thin slices of brioche
butter
icing sugar (optional)

1. Turn on the oven to 180°C/350°F/Gas 4.

2. Butter the slices of brioche. Lay on a flat non-stick baking tray.

3. Bake for 3 or 4 minutes, until lightly toasted.

When it comes to dishing up, put one brioche slice on each plate. Divide up the rhubarb bits among them, and plonk the matching brioche slice on top. Dust with icing sugar for fancy effect, and serve with rhubarb ice cream. You could, of course, turn it into an open Danish-effect sandwich by not putting the second slice on top.

Rhubarb Ice Cream

I just love the richness of the cream calming down the exuberant rhubarb in this recipe.

2 eggs
115g caster sugar
285ml double cream
115ml full-cream milk
2tsp vanilla essence
rhubarb juice from recipes above

1. Break the eggs into a bowl and add the sugar. Beat for 1
   minute if using an electric beater, for 2 minutes if doing
   it by hand.

2. Add the cream, and beat for a further 20 seconds.

3. Add the milk and beat for another 20 seconds.

4. Add the vanilla essence and the rhubarb juice.

5. Decant the whole lot into your ice-cream machine and
   let it do its job until the ice cream is made.

6. If you have to make it by hand, put the mixture into a plastic
   container and put the plastic container into your freezer.
   Give a thorough stir every 20 minutes or so until frozen.

❧ making an effort ❧

Aubergine and Mozzarella Sandwiches in Beer Tempura

Crisp batter, as light as a rime of frost, squidgy aubergine,
squidgier mozzarella – you can see how this works, can't you?
You could do worse than wash it down with more of the beer
you used to make the batter.

8 aubergines
plain flour
olive oil
250g mozzarella
150g more plain flour
1 tsp salt
½ tsp black pepper
375ml Nastro Azzuro (or some other light beer)
750ml vegetable oil

1. Slice the aubergines thinly, then dip in the flour and fry
    in olive oil until golden brown. Drain on kitchen towel.

2. Slice the mozzarella thinly and place a layer on half of the
    aubergines. Put the other aubergine slices on top to make
    a sandwich. Press down firmly. Put 2 toothpicks through each
    to hold together.

3. Chill the beer well. Put the plain flour, salt and pepper in
    a bowl. Add the beer gradually, beating all the time until
    you have a smooth batter about as thick as a thin cream.

4. Put the vegetable oil into a saucepan and bring to
    smoking point.

5. Dip each aubergine sandwich in the batter and transfer
    straight to the oil. Fry until the batter is just turning brown.
    You will have to do them in batches. Do not overload the
    fat or it will cool down, and disaster (i.e. soggy coating)
    will result. Drain on kitchen towel and hand them out
    while still piping hot.

Carpaccio of Sea Bream and Pomegranates with Hazelnut Oil

I first had carpaccio in 1988 in Milan. It was the classic beef carpaccio cut as thin as Brussels lace, buried beneath a blizzard of white truffle. Both phrases were enough to land me in Pseuds Corner in Private Eye, something that gave a number of my friends a good deal of pleasure. Not as much pleasure as the dish gave me, however. I have tinkered with the basic idea ever since. The inspiration for this combination came from lunch in a restaurant in Venice which went on so long and was so pleasurable that I am quite unable to remember the name of the establishment. The jewels of pomegranate bring a lively acidity to the raw fish, and are prettier than using lemon juice.

225g sea bream
(or other similar, firm-fleshed fish – turbot, halibut, sea bass, monkfish)
salt and pepper
1 pomegranate
1dsp hazelnut oil
1 small bunch parsley
1 small bunch mint

1. Very carefully cut slices off the fillet, angling the knife slightly downwards and cutting towards the tail. Cut as thinly as you can. It doesn't matter if some slices are bigger than others.

2. Lay each slice onto the plate you want your lucky guests to eat it off. Just keep on slicing and dividing up until the fillet has all gone.

3. Season each plate of carpaccio lightly with salt and pepper.

4. Squeeze the juice from one half of the pomegranate over the plates, and then dribble just a few drops of hazelnut oil over them.

5. Scoop the seeds from the other half of the pomegranate
    and scatter a few over each plate.

6. Chop the parsley and mint finely and do likewise.
    Serve right away.

Crab and Parmesan Crisp Stack

Parmesan crisps have a vital part to play in the display side
of cooking, because they are very easy to make, look very
stylish, pack a considerable punch and are endlessly versatile.
Cheese and crab is one of the more terrific combinations.

120g grated Parmesan
400g fresh white crab meat
lemon juice
pepper
1 bunch parsley
olive oil

1. Turn on the oven to 190°C/375°F/Gas 5.

2. On a baking sheet (those new-fangled, high-tech nonstick
    sheets are the best) form a series of discs about 5cm across
    with the Parmesan. I use a biscuit cutter for the purposes.
    Just divide up the Parmesan between them. You will need
    12 crisps in all.

3. Put into the oven, and bake until the Parmesan has melted
    and gone a pale, wheaty brown – about 5 minutes, but check
    before to make sure.

4. Take out of the oven and cool. When they are quite cold
    you will find that they have become crisp.

5. Put the crab meat into a bowl. Season with pepper and lemon juice.

6. Finely chop the parsley and add that to crab.

7. Place a dollop of crab meat in the middle of a plate.

8. Place a Parmesan crisp on top. Build the stack, finishing with a Parmesan crisp.

9. Dribble a little olive oil around and a squeeze or two of lemon juice.

Pea Mousse with Shrimp Cream

A fancier dish for a summer's day.

2 shallots
50g unsalted butter
400g peas (fresh or frozen)
250ml double cream
3 eggs
salt and pepper

1. Turn on the oven to 170°C/325°F/Gas 3.

2. Finely dice the shallots.

3. Heat the butter in a saucepan and fry the shallots until they turn a pale gold.

4. Throw in the peas. Add a couple of tablespoons of water if using frozen peas, about 115ml stock if using fresh peas. Cook for 3 to 4 minutes.

5. Scrape the peas and liquid into a food processor or blender. Add the cream and whizz up until smooth. Taste. Season.

6. Add the eggs and whizz again. Butter 4 ramekins or one large dish.

7. Pour the mousse mixture into them/it. Put in a roasting tray with a piece of folded newspaper underneath (to promote even cooking).

8. Pour boiling water into the pan until it comes ¾-way up the side of the mousse holders. Cover with loose greaseproof paper or foil and cook in the oven for 35 to 40 minutes. You can tell when they are ready by sticking a knife into one of them – if it comes out clean, they are done. Turn them out and surround with the shrimp cream (see below).

For the Shrimp Cream
1 small onion
1 stick celery
2tbsp olive oil
200g cooked Atlantic prawns
115ml white wine
2tbsp double cream
salt and pepper

1. Finely chop the onion and celery.

2. Heat the oil in a saucepan. When mazy, add the onion and celery and fry until soft, about 5 minutes.

3. Add the prawns, shells and all.

4. Add the wine. Bring to a simmering point and cook for 20 minutes.

5. Pour the contents into a food processor and blast to bits.

6. Pass through a sieve into a clean pan and season.

7. Reheat and add the cream.

Watercress and Scallop Soup

I had to feed a couple of friends who decided to turn up with
minimal warning one evening. The trouble is that I had bought
scallops for two, and was faced with the challenge of stretching
them, as they say in the trade. The watercress turned out to be
the medium. That peppery flavour worked very nicely with the
scallops, and those white coins of shellfish stood out against
the dark soup rather fetchingly, too.

4 spring onions
1 carrot
200g floury potatoes (eg. Cara, Golden Wonder, King Edward,
Maris Piper, Pentland Crown)
40g unsalted butter
1 litre chicken stock
150ml Chambery vermouth
1 bunch of parsley
2 large bunches of watercress
lemon juice
4 fat scallops
olive oil

1. Peel and dice the potatoes, dice the carrots finely and slice
   the onions, including the green part, finely.

2. Melt the butter in a pan.

3. Stew the potatoes, carrots and onions for 10 minutes very gently.

4. Add the stock and vermouth and cook until the vegetables
   are tender, another 10 minutes or so.

5. Add the parsley and watercress and turn over briefly in the juices.

6. Blast the whole lot in a blender until smooth. Pass through a sieve to give the soup that silky appeal. Add a dash of lemon juice to sharpen up the flavours.

7. Slice the scallops across into 3 thin slices (or in half if you can't manage that).

8. Heat 2tbsp of olive oil in a frying pan until smoking.

9. Throw in the scallop slices. Give them 10 seconds on either side.

10. Divide up the soup between four plates and carefully place the scallop slices on top. Serve immediately.

Sea Bass with Sorrel Sauce

A.k.a. bar a l'oseille, a classic of the Norman kitchen.

2 shallots
55g butter
115g sorrel
115ml white wine or, better still, Chambery vermouth
115ml whipping cream
8 sea bass fillets

1. Finely chop the shallots and cook in the butter in a saucepan until soft.

2. Add the sorrel and the white wine and boil hard until the white wine/vermouth has reduced by half.

3. Whip the cream and fold into the sorrel/wine sludge.

4. Fry the sea bass fillets bottom-side down in a nonstick pan wiped with a little vegetable oil until it is cooked most of the way through – about 6 to 8 minutes.

5. Flip over and brown the top side.

6. Serve with the sorrel sauce and a potato or two.

Pheasant with Cabbage and White Wine

The pheasant can tend to dryness (and can be low key in the flavour department, unless you are lucky enough to get them properly hung). But braising them in a duvet of white cabbage (white cabbage because it can take a lot of cooking and still keep some texture) and the other flavourings really gives the pheasant a boost in both departments.

2 pheasants
50g butter
2 large white cabbages
1 tsp black peppercorns
1 tsp juniper berries
2 tbsp white vinegar
250ml white wine
30g butter
salt and pepper

1. Season the pheasants inside with plenty of salt and pepper.

2. Heat the butter in a frying pan. When it is foaming, brown the pheasants as best as you can all over.

3. Cut the core out of the cabbages and slice it up thinly.

4. Put half in the bottom of a casserole and toss in the spices.

5. Place the pheasants on top. Season.

6. Cover with the rest of the cabbage, then pour the vinegar and wine in.

7. Bring to simmering point and simmer away for about 40 minutes. The pheasants should be cooked but not reduced to a dry and withered state.

8. Pour off the juices and taste. Reduce if you think necessary. Beat in the butter.

9. Heap the cabbage onto a large plate. Carve up the pheasants and pile on top. Serve the buttery juices separately.

Roast Duck with Cider Sauce and Rillettes Potatoes

Something for a big occasion. It may seem like a lot of work, but it isn't really, and most of the serious stuff can be done well in advance. Incidentally, the thinking behind cooking the duck breast on the bone is because the bone holds the breast in shape while it cooks, and stops it from shrivelling down to half its size and becoming as tough as old boots.

The breasts
1 good-sized (3.5-4kg) duck
salt and pepper

1. Pre-heat the oven to 200°C/400°F/Gas 6.

2. Cut the legs and wings off the carcass. Using a heavy knife or cleaver, cut off the undercarriage, all the base of the duck, leaving the crown – the breast of the bird – in one piece.

3. Chop up the undercarriage roughly.

4. Place the breast in a lightly oiled frying pan, skin-side down, and place over a high heat to brown.

5. When golden-amber, slip into the oven for 10 minutes.

6. Take out of the oven and allow to cool. You can do this earlier in the day or even the day before if you want.

7. When you need to serve it, carve the two breasts off the bone and reheat gently in the sauce (see below); that way any juices flowing out of the meat are reincorporated into the sauce.

The sauce
2tbsp olive oil
duck bits and bobs
1 medium onion
1 medium carrot
1 stick celery
1 bay leaf
1tsp black peppercorns
500ml cider
salt

1. Heat the oil in a saucepan until smoking.

2. Throw in the duck bits, including the wings, and brown them.

3. Cut the onion and carrot into quarters and break the celery stick in half.

4. Put into the pan, and turn in the hot fat.

5. Add the bay leaf, peppercorns and cider. If the cider doesn't cover the contents of the pan, add more cider or water until it does.

6. Turn down the heat and simmer for 1 to 1½ hours.

7. Strain the liquid into a fresh saucepan and reduce until it gets to the intensity you like. Season with salt.

The rillettes potatoes
2 duck legs
salt and pepper
bunch of thyme (optional)
250g potatoes
duck fat

1. Turn down the oven to 140°C/275°F/Gas 1 and confit the legs as described in Chapter 6.

2. When the flesh is falling off the bone, help it on its way and shred it with two forks.

3. Sprinkle with salt and pepper, and some thyme leaves if you have any. Keep warm until needed.

4. Peel the potatoes, and cut into really small chunks, 2-3mm square. The size is really important.

5. Heat the fat the legs have left behind until really hot and fry the potato in it until brown and crisp.

6. Take out and drain on kitchen towel. Keep warm.

7. When it comes to serving, mix the potatoes and shredded duck and divide between the plates.

Braised Shoulder of Lamb

Shoulder has been a favourite cut of mine for a long time. It's not as comely as a leg, or as easy to carve, but the extra fat and connective tissue keeps it succulent during long cooking, and gives it a couple of fields more flavour. And because you have cooked it long and slow, it becomes so soft and tender, you can practically eat it with a spoon.

1 onion
1 carrot
2 celery stalks
1 shoulder of lamb with all fat trimmed off
whole head of garlic
2tbsp white-wine vinegar
1 bottle white wine
2 bay leaves
a big bunch of thyme
1dsp black peppercorns
olive oil
salt

1. Preheat the oven to 180°C/350°F/Gas 4.

2. Roughly chop the onion, carrot and celery.

3. Heat 2tbsp oil in a casserole or roasting pan large enough to take the shoulder. Brown the vegetables in the hot fat – about 10 minutes.

4. Add the shoulder, vinegar, wine, garlic, bay leaves and peppercorns. Pop the lid of the casserole on or cover with 2 layers of foil and slide into the oven for 2 hours.

5. Half an hour before the end of cooking, take off the casserole lid or foil and turn up the oven to 200°C/400°F/Gas 6. This will have the effect of browning the top of the shoulder and reducing the bubbling liquid. At the end of 2 hours, the meat should just lift away from the bone.

6. Pour off this liquid into a saucepan, let it settle for 5 minutes

or so, and then spoon off as much fat as you can.

7. Taste the fat-free liquid, and if it isn't strong enough for your liking, boil it down until it is.

8. Plunge the bunch of thyme into the remaining juices and infuse of 5 to 10 minutes.

9. Evacuate the head of garlic and squeeze soft flesh onto a plate and mash up. Add the mashed garlic to the juices.

Cabbage Stuffed with Cardamom Rice

I have to be truthful. I am second to none in my love of vegetables but I am not at ease with vegetarian food. Nothing to do with ideological differences. It's just that I'm a lazy cook and it requires more energy and imagination than I have to create masterful vegetarian dishes. Just occasionally I respond to the call, however.

1 Savoy or January King cabbage
150g basmati rice
3 sticks celery
3 leeks, white part only
3 medium carrots
olive oil or butter
1 tsp mustard seeds
2 tbsp pine kernels
2 tbsp sultanas
1 tsp cardamom
2 eggs
salt and pepper

1. Take 12 of the outer leaves off the cabbage and blanch for 4 minutes in boiling water. Cool and refresh in cold water. Dry thoroughly.

2. Chop the rest of the cabbage quite roughly. Cook in the same water until soft. Drain and squeeze out as much retained water as possible.

3. Cook the rice as per instructions. Drain thoroughly.

4. Chop the other vegetables very finely.

5. Heat the oil or butter in a pan, then add the mustard seeds.

6. As they begin to pop, add the chopped vegetables and stew in the oil or butter over a low heat until soft, about 10 minutes.

7. Add the cabbage, rice, sultanas and cardamom pods and cook for another 2 minutes. Season to taste.

8. Toast the pine nuts in a pan until lightly browned.

9. Let the mixture cool slightly before adding the pine nuts and beating in the eggs.

10. Lay out a piece of clingfilm roughly 30cm square.

11. Cut the thickest part of the rib out of each cabbage leaf. Lay 3 cabbage leaves in a clover shape, overlapping each other, in the centre of the clingfilm. You should have a slightly irregular cabbage circle.

12. Plop one-sixth of the vegetable mixture in the centre of the cabbage leaves.

13. Pick up the 4 corners of the clingfilm and carefully draw them towards each other. This should cause the cabbage leaves to wrap themselves around the filling. Twirl the corners of the clingfilm together, sealing everything inside, making a neat, plump, circular package.

14. Repeat for the other 3 helpings. If you don't fancy using clingfilm, use muslin or even a J-cloth. This can all be done well in advance.

15. Just keep them in the fridge until you are ready to finish the cooking by steaming them or poaching them in salted water for 15 to 20 minutes.

Mashed Broad Beans

I hate throwing any food away. Even mealy old broad beans have their uses if you can be bothered to take a little trouble with them, in this case a very little trouble.

800g podded old broad beans
250ml chicken stock
juice of ½ lemon
1 small bunch of parsley
2tbsp double cream
salt and pepper

1. Put the broad beans into a pan and cover with the stock.

2. Boil until the beans are well cooked – 15 minutes, I would say. If you are really finicky, you will now squeeze the brilliant, emerald-green centres out of their wrinkled, greyish skins. I am not finicky. I like the deep-down and earthy flavour the skins have.

3. Bung the whole beans into the food processor along with the remains of the stock, lemon juice and parsley, and blast them to a purée.

4. Turn the purée out into a saucepan, season with salt and pepper, beat in the cream and gently reheat.

OK, French beans are fine, although they've usually come a very long way to get to us, but really they pale into insignificance alongside the grassy freshness of our own runner beans when the season is high. You may have to cheat a bit on the wild-mushroom side to maintain seasonal purity, but chanterelles should be about.

400g runner beans
300g wild mushrooms (preferably chanterelle)
55g butter
salt and pepper
1 bunch flat-leaf parsley

1. Top, tail and slice the runner beans.

2. Bring a pot of unsalted water to the boil.

3. Plunge the beans in, clap on the lid and boil until cooked through. Drain. Plunge into cold water. Drain again.

4. Carefully pick over the wild mushrooms to remove any grass or leafy debris, but do not wash.

5. Heat the butter in a frying pan. When the butter is smoking, throw in the mushrooms. Turn down the heat and stew until soft and tender – about 7 to 8 minutes.

6. Before serving, add the beans and heat until everything is nice and hot. Season with salt and pepper.

7. Chop the parsley finely and scatter all over.

Prosciutto and Potato Pie

A development of a development of an idea I first came across in Memories of Gascony by the great Pierre Koffman. It goes surprisingly well with roast beef, oddly enough, or the roast duck (above). Or almost anything.

500g potatoes
pepper
2x80g packets of cured ham (or 12 slices in all)
butter

1. Turn on the oven to 170°C/325°F/Gas 3.

2. Peel and slice the potatoes. The slices should be about 1cm thick.

3. Blanch them in salted boiling water for 2 minutes. Drain and cool, then season with pepper only (the ham should take care of the salty bit).

4. Butter the inside of a frying pan. Cover the bottom and sides with slices of ham. The ends of the slices should flop over the side of the frying pan.

5. Pour the blanched, sliced potato into the pan and arrange evenly all over. Flip the ham ends over the potato and cover the top with any remaining slices of ham.

6. Bake in the oven for 30 minutes. Slice it like a cake.

Zabaglione with Oranges

Let's face it, Italian cooking is not overendowed with great puddings. But then no country is, compared with Britain. One of the few Italian puddings that can genuinely challenge for a place at the top table, in my view, is zabaglione. I have added some bits of orange to keep it healthy. And those sharp explosions of fruit contrast nicely with the rich foam of the beaten egg yolks.

2 oranges
6 egg yolks
3tbsp caster sugar
150ml marsala

1. Peel the oranges and cut into individual segments. Keep to one side.

2. Separate the eggs. Keep the whites for another occasion.

3. Put the yolks into a bain-marie over simmering water.

4. Add the sugar and begin whisking them all up. When the sugar gets to the pale and interesting stage, pour in the marsala.

5. Keep on beating until the zabaglione is airy and frothy.

6. Divide the zabaglione up between warm plates.

7. Drop the orange segments on top at random.

Chocolate Soufflé with Mars Bar

Once upon a time I was asked to cook a dinner for a hen party, believe it or not. Make it really sexy, I was told. I can't remember too much about it, except for a dish of sea bass fillets in a cream sauce and topped with caviar. The pudding did live to see several more incarnations. The Mars bar was an early version of those chocolate puds with cakey outsides and liquid centres you see everywhere. The deep-frozen nugget melts as the soufflé cooks, delivering, as modern argot has it, a terrific sugar hit as you spoon it into your mouth.

1 Mars bar
40g butter
100g finest dark chocolate
1dsp instant coffee dissolved in 1½ tbsp water
20g corn- or rice-flour
190ml full milk
20g caster sugar
3 egg yolks
4 egg whites
Pinch of salt
icing sugar

1. Divide the Mars bar into 4 pieces and put in the freezer for
   20 minutes or so.

2. Turn on the oven to 190°C/375°F/Gas 5.

3. Melt 20g butter and use it to butter 1 large soufflé bowl
   or 4 ramekins.

4. Break up the chocolate into pieces and put into a pan along
   with the coffee. Heat over a low flame or heat until the
   chocolate is melted. Remove from the heat and keep warm
   (i.e. over hot water) until needed.

5. In a saucepan beat the corn- or rice-flour with 3tbsp cold
   milk until blended and smooth.

6. Beat in the rest of the cold milk and the sugar.

7. Put the pan on the hob and, over a moderate heat, stir the
   mixture until it hits boiling point. Boil briefly. It should be
   very gluey.

8. Turn off the heat and add the melted chocolate, stirring until
   it is well mixed.
9. Add the 3 egg yolks, beating them well in.

10. In a bowl beat the egg whites with a pinch of salt until they are at the soft-peak stage. Add the rest of the sugar and go on beating until stiff.

11. Carefully stir one-third of the stiff egg whites into the chocolate base. Fold in the rest.

12. Turn half the soufflé mixture into the soufflé dish or divide up among the ramekins. If using one soufflé dish place a layer of the Mars bar bits across the middle, or pop one into each ramekin. Either way, cover with the rest of the chocolate soufflé mixture.

13. Slide the soufflé(s) into the oven and bake for 25 minutes (ramekins) or 40 minutes (soufflé dish). Dust with icing sugar.

5. now we are six

Unless you have an unusually large family, cooking for six means
that you'll be cooking for friends, neighbours, odds, sods and
others. Cooking for six means a bit of thought, a bit of planning,
a bit of effort, a bit of washing up. Can't be helped. That's the
way it is. If you don't fancy any of those things, stop reading
here, and don't go around inviting friends, neighbours, odds,
sods or others again.

If you are a convivial sort, however, six is just the foothills of the
sunny uplands of cooking at home, when the sound of laughter
and appreciation roll out from your table through the house.
I must say, I'm of the latter persuasion. I remember once, having
slipped away from the table during dinner for a pee, coming
back down the stairs and hearing this wall of sound consisting
of conversation, laughter and debate. That's what it's all about,
I thought. That's why I do it.

You see, you can have the finest food in the world lubricated
by some of the world's grandest wines, and if the company
is dire, it will be ashes in the mouth. And you can have a supper
of, say, pasta and chickpea soup, chicken with elderflower and

carrots and pears braised in perry and honey washed down with a modest pinot grigio in the company of people you love, and you will remember it for the rest of your life. Good food, even great food, won't make an occasion memorable on its own. Happiness at the table begins and ends with company. Food can help build on that.

So now we are six. Let's see what we can do.

ঙ a piece of cake ঙ

Ricotta with Orange and Lemon Peel and Mint

This began life as nibble I developed after I had been tempted into an impulse buy of some goats' curd. Goats' curd not being universally available, I've changed the main ingredient to the more common ricotta (now there's an odd thing) and tinkered with the recipe, too. It just needs some good bread to round things out.

1 organic or unwaxed lemon
1 organic or unwaxed orange
250g ricotta
bunch of mint
salt and pepper

1. Grate the peel on a fine grater. Chop the mint leaves.

2. Mix with goats' curd or ricotta. Season.

3. Leave to stand for at least an hour.

4. Using 2 dessertspoons, scoop out an appropriate amount of

the mixture, shape into a quenelle like a rugby ball and pop into the centre of a small plate.

You don't need a lot of this soup. It's on what you might call the filling side. The trouble is, you may be tempted to a second helping because it's so delicious. Don't give in if you want to eat much afterwards. It's very popular in Naples (actually very popular throughout Italy in various versions).

200g chickpeas
2 cloves garlic
1 small hot chilli – fresh or dry
2 celery stalks
2 large tomatoes
150ml extra-virgin olive oil
1 litre water
300g pasta bits
salt and pepper
basil leaves

1. Cover the chickpeas with cold water and soak overnight. Discard the water. Transfer the chickpeas to a saucepan and cover with water. Bring to the boil and cook for 2 hours until soft. Drain.

2. Finely chop the garlic, chilli and celery. Peel, deseed and chop the tomatoes.

3. In a second pan heat the oil until hot.

4. Throw in the garlic, chilli, celery and tomatoes and cook for 3 to 4 minutes. Do not let the garlic colour.

5. Toss in the chickpeas and roll around until well coated.

Add the water and pasta and continue heating over a gentle flame for 10 minutes.

6. Season with salt to suit your taste.

7. Tear up the basil leaves and straw in. Serve right away with a bit more olive oil dribbled over the top.

Onions and Potatoes Fried in Duck Fat with Duck Eggs

Everything cooked in duck fat tastes better. Don't ask me why. It just does. The Gascons certainly believe so. They cook everything in duck fat, and they have the lowest rates of heart disease in Europe. It's known as the Gascon Paradox in medical circles. Perhaps we don't eat enough duck fat.

600g onions
400g potatoes
100g duck fat
1 tbsp cider vinegar
6 duck eggs
medium-sized bunch of parsley
salt and pepper

1. Slice the onions finely. Dice the potatoes into not too small bits.

2. Melt 75g of the duck fat in a frying pan.

3. When fizzing with heat, add the onions, turn down the heat and cook gently for 20 minutes, until sweet, soft and golden. Turn them out of the pan onto a plate or some such, season with salt and pepper and keep warm.

4. Turn up the heat under the pan again and throw in the potatoes.

5. Fry until caramelised on either side, about 5 minutes, turning them over from time to time. Add the onions back again and toss in the cider vinegar. Continue frying until the vinegar has been absorbed.

6. Chop the parsley finely and add. Season, remove from the pan and keep warm.

7. Melt the remaining 25g duck fat in the frying pan. When sizzling, break in the duck eggs, making sure you spread them out all over the base of the frying pan.

8. Fry until the whites are firm. Put a small mound of onions and mushrooms on each plate and cap with a fried egg, and serve.

Cucumber and Prawn Salad

I have to admit that onions and potatoes fried in duck fat may not be everyone's idea of a fine summer dish, so here's something for anyone looking for a light, bright number for warmer days. I strongly suggest using Atlantic prawns. In fact, I'd go further, and say that you ought to buy the ones in their shells. They have so much more sweet, briny flavour than farmed tiger prawns or even ready-peeled Atlantic ones. Look, I know it's a bit fiddly, but your guests will really appreciate it, and you can use the shells to make a spectacular sauce for fish.

2 cucumbers
2tbsp extra-virgin olive oil
1tsp lemon juice
100ml double cream
1tsp paprika or cayenne pepper
salt
500g peeled Atlantic prawns
1 bunch of dill

1. Peel, deseed and slice the cucumber into batons (i.e. pieces about 4cm long and half as thick as a pencil).

2. Mix the olive oil, lemon juice, paprika and cream.

3. Mix the prawns and cucumber batons in a bowl. Season with salt and cayenne or paprika.

4. Pour the dressing over the salad.

5. Chop the dill and scatter on top.

6. Let it rest for 15 minutes before serving.

Squid with Celery and Fennel Salsa

Sweet, firm squid, crunchy celery and fennel. Breezy, zingy lemon juice. Soothing, grassy olive oil. Cool salsa. Hot chilli. You can see how it works.

2 fennel bulbs
6 sticks celery
extra-virgin olive oil
juice of 1-1½ lemons
salt and pepper
600g squid
2 small red chillies

1. Chop the celery and the fennel finely, including any celery leaves and fennel fronds.

2. Dress with olive oil, lemon juice and then season.

3. Clean and slice the squid into thin strips.

4. Chop the chillies.

5. Heat some olive oil in a frying pan until smoking. Hurl in the squid strips and the chillies. Fry for 30 seconds, then flick over or stir about. Give them another 30 seconds and tip them out.

6. Divide up the salsa in heaps between the plates and plonk the squid strips beside it.

Potato Salad with Capers

A kind of Saturday-lunch filler, this needs to be part of a bigger picture – cold chicken, belly pork, cold sausages. Something like that. Actually, it's good with fish as well. The capers give a merry sharpness, you see. I have included a recipe for mayonnaise for anyone who wants to make their own, although you can buy some halfway decent ready-made ones.

680g waxy potatoes
(e.g. Pink Fir Apple, Charlotte, Belle de Fontenay, Nicola)
140ml caper mayonnaise (see below)

1. Bring some water to the boil and add the potatoes in their skins. Cook until they are just cooked through. (The length of time will depend on: a) the size of potato, b) the variety of potato, c) the age of the potato. You just have to keep testing.) Drain.

2. When cool enough, peel and cut into slices 1cm thick. And only peel if you feel the need.

3. Make the caper mayonnaise (see below) or add the capers to a bought mayonnaise, keeping a few back for surface decoration.

4. Add the potato slices to the caper mayonnaise, letting them finish cooling in there for a couple of hours. Scatter the capers you've kept back over the top.

Caper mayonnaise

1 egg
1 tsp Dijon mustard
½ tsp salt
1 tbsp lemon juice
50g capers
300ml olive oil

1. Whiz up the egg, mustard, salt, lemon juice and most of the capers in a food processor or blender for 15 seconds or so.

2. Go on whizzing while you pour in the olive oil in a thin stream.

Rocket, Chicory and Pear Salad

The pear is a fruit. It has about one day when it is perfect. One day too early, it's hard and dry. One day late and it's a loathsome woolly mush. But get it right, there is no finer fruit: sweet, perfumes, juice, exquisite. It may seem a bit of a waste in that case, to put it into a salad, but I think not. You must make this and eat it right away. Peeled pears do not take kindly to being kept waiting.

2 ripe pears (Comice or Williams, or Conference at a pinch)
lemon juice
3 heads of chicory
1 large bunch of rocket
extra-virgin olive oil

1. Peel, core and slice up the pear. Squeeze the lemon juice over the slices to stop them going brown.

2. Cut the chicory crossways into bits about 2cm wide. Put the chicory bits into a bowl. Delicately mix in the pear slices and then the rocket.

3. Splash olive oil generously all over and season with salt and pepper.

Mutton and Barley Stew

I am a great believer in simplicity. It makes things easy for the cook. Take this stew. You don't even have to brown the meat. But it has a lovely clear flavour as well as the delicious mushroomy chewiness of the barley. Mutton has been making something of a comeback, which I am all in favour of encouraging. The sheep get to live longer for a start, and we get to eat sheep with a bit more texture and flavour than perhaps we have been used to. Of course you can use lamb, but make sure it's end-of-season lamb. You need that boom-boom that age gives.

2 large onions
6 carrots
50g barley
1kg mutton chops (neck/scrag end if possible)
salt and pepper

1. Chop the onions none too finely. Slice the carrots.

2. Put into a casserole dish along with the barley and meat, then cover with water, bring to the simmer and simmer away for 1 to 1½ hours until the meat is tender.

3. Season and allow to cool overnight.

4. Reheat the next day.

Naturally, not one to be served on its own. It will go with pork recipes below, roast beef possibly, or venison (see Chapter 6).

300g large carrots
300g peeled chestnuts
1 bay leaf
1 sprig of rosemary
1 tsp black peppercorns
1 tsp unsalted butter
100ml marsala

1. Peel and chop up the carrots into large chunks – about half the length of your thumb and the same thickness. Place them in a saucepan with the chestnuts.

2. Add the herbs, peppercorns, butter and marsala. Add enough water so that the vegetables are just covered.

3. Bring to simmering point and cook away for 15 minutes.

4. At this point, the liquid should have almost evaporated, leaving the vegetables glossy and tender. If either of these conditions has not been arrived at, either go on cooking until the veg are cooked, tender and glossy; or take them out and boil down the liquid until it is fit to become a glaze and put the vegetables back in to be glazed.

Pears Braised in Perry and Honey

As you can see, I have a soft spot for pears. This time they shouldn't be too ripe or they will simply fall apart during the cooking. Perry is cider made with pears, so there is a happy reunion going on.

6 Conference pears
½ a lemon
¼ stick cinnamon
2 cloves
10 black peppercorns
1 bottle of perry
1dsp runny honey

1. Peel the pears and slice in half. Rub each with the lemon as you do so.

2. Place the pear halves and spices in a saucepan. Then pour in the perry and honey.

3. Bring to simmering point and simmer until the halves can be easily pierced with a knife.

4. Allow to cool in the juice.

5. When cool, pour off the juice into a separate pan, straining off the spices, and reduce to a thick, rich syrup.

6. Pour back over the pears and keep until ready to serve. Serve with cream and a buttery shortbread biscuit.

✌ no sweat ✌

Broad Bean, Feta and Savory Salad

Shakespeare said that troubles come not singly, but in battalions. It's the same with broad beans. Luckily, I love them. When I make this recipe at home, I pick the very youngest, earliest beans, and don't bother to cook them. Unless you are a broad-bean fan like me and grow your own, you probably won't be able to follow this counsel of perfection, so you had better cook them first. Savory is the classic herb to go with broad beans. It has a distinctive peppery, lemony flavour. If you can find it, try mint instead. Of course it's completely different, but nice all the same.

1kg broad beans
400g feta
½ a lemon
olive oil
sprigs of savory
pepper

1. Pod and cook the broad beans in lots of boiling water.

2. Drain them and plunge into cold water. You can take them out of their grey skins if you want to be really meticulous, but I wouldn't bother.

3. Cut the feta cheese into similar shapes but slightly smaller.

4. Squeeze the lemon over them, sprinkle with olive oil and dust with pepper (salt is not necessary because the feta is salty).

5. Strip the leaves off the savory sprigs and scatter all over.

Piadina Romagnola Stuffed with Sausage and Spinach

Street food of Emilia Romagna, that bit of Italy on the right-hand side just below Venice and the Veneto. Very keen on their grub, the Emiliani and Romagnoli. I first came across this one day when I was chilled to the marrow after a morning in the saddle of my Vespa, riding through cold rain with inadequate protection. I was very cheered. You might be, too.

Piadina
250g '00' flour
2tsp sugar
salt
50g pork fat or 2-3tbsp olive oil
milk

1. Mix the dry ingredients.

2. Add the fat or oil and enough milk to make a soft dough.
    Knead briefly.

3. Rest in a cool place for 1 hour.

4. Divide up the dough into 6 and roll each out into rounds
    about 25cm across.

5. Fry each piadina on an old-fashioned pancake griddle or a
    nonstick pan lubricated with a little more pork fat or olive
    oil. Give them 2 minutes on each side.

6. Flip onto a board. Fill with whatever you fancy. Fold over and
    eat in your fingers.

Filling
6 bangers
olive oil
1 clove garlic
500g spinach
lemon juice
salt and pepper

1. Fry the sausages slowly until nice and brown.

2. Take out of the pan and cut into thinnish slices.

3. Add a little oil to the frying pan and the peeled garlic clove.

4. Fry until golden brown and discard.

5. Add the spinach and fry gently until thoroughly wilted.

6. Squeeze some lemon juice over it, and season with black pepper.

7. Divide up between the piadine, fold over, then eat in your fingers.

Salmon with Broad Beans, Pancetta and Cider

Oops, another broad-bean recipe. Never mind. You can't have too much of a good thing. Or use peas if you're fed up with beans. Incidentally, I would only ever cook organic salmon (assuming I couldn't catch or find a wild one). Organic has at least some of the muscular denseness, colour and taste of the real thing. The rest I wouldn't feed to my dogs.

150g unsmoked pancetta or bacon
1 onion
55g butter
115ml sweet cider
6 organic salmon steaks
600g broad beans (out of their pods)
salt and pepper

1. Chop the onion and pancetta or bacon.

2. Melt the butter in a frying pan large enough to take all the salmon steaks – a sauté pan would be even better.

3. Fry the onion and the pancetta/bacon until the fat runs from it and the onion is transparent.

4. Pour the cider into the pan and stir up all the bits stuck to the bottom.

5. Place the salmon steaks on top of the onion and bacon, and if you have a lid that fits over the pan, pop it on. If not, cover with foil, and cook the salmon like this for 10 to 15 minutes. Check that they are cooked through and season.

6. In another pan bring some unsalted water to the boil, and pour the broad beans into the water. Cook for just a minute or two if they are really young, a little longer if they are older. Drain.

7. Remove the salmon steaks from the onion/pancetta/cider and keep warm.

8. Add the broad beans to the onion/pancetta/cider and stir round. Check seasoning. The dish is now ready to serve, although you could add a potato or two to bulk it up.

Risotto Alla Pilota with Pork and Sausage Meat

The pilota was the chap who flayed the rice in the areas between Vercelli, Novara and Mantua, known as the rice triangle. Clearly he was an important bloke because he had a dish named after him, although it is extremely non-labour intensive to prepare. Actually, it produces a risotto more like a pilau than the creamy thing I normally think of when I see the word. I had it first in an old-fashioned watermill called Il Galleoto outside Mantua. There was a terrific restaurant where the mill's admirable products were cooked. I had two risotti, this, and one flavoured with tiny deep-fried fish. The fish had been caught in the little streams and channels that surrounded the paddy fields, not an option open to most of us.

50g butter
1 onion finely chopped
300g pork, cut into small cubes
300g sausage meat

water – the locals will tell you that you need the same quantity of rice to water, plus half a cup for the pot
350g Vialone Nano rice
salt
Parmesan

1. Melt the butter in a pan.

2. Fry the sausage meat, pork and onion until cooked and the pork is tender.

3. In another pot, bring the water to the boil.

4. Pour the rice into the boiling water all at once to form a pyramid with its top just below the surface of the water. Shake the pan gently to collapse the pyramid.

5. Add a little salt. Put the top on the pan, and cook very gently for 10 minutes. Turn off the heat and let it stand for another 10 minutes. The rice should have absorbed all the water, and be quite dry.

6. Stir in a good deal of grated Parmesan and then the pork. Serve immediately.

Chicken with Elderflower and Carrots

This has become something of a staple in the Fort family, and in a number of other homes as well. I don't know what it is, but chicken and elderflower seem to go together like Astaire & Rogers or Rodgers & Hammerstein. Rogers & Grey, come to that. (That's Ruth Rogers and Rose Grey of the River Café. I can never resist a verbal flourish).You may need two chickens for six people, depending on the size of the chickens, in which case up the quantities. I get large chickens, and very tasty they are too.

1 chicken
(or buy enough legs and breasts already cut up to make the recipe)
75g butter
600g carrots
1 onion
2 sticks celery
150ml elderflower cordial
250ml chicken stock
4 tbsp olive oil
peel and juice of ½ lemon
salt and pepper

1. Cut the chicken into 2 legs, 2 thighs, and 4 bits of breast (i.e. cut the breastbone in half lengthways, between the breasts, and then cut each breast in half).

2. Heat half the butter and the olive oil in a frying pan and, when just short of smoking, brown each of the chicken pieces as thoroughly as possible. Transfer to a dish as each bit browns and keep warm.

3. Dice the onion and celery and slice the carrots as thinly as possible.

4. Melt the rest of the butter in a casserole and add the onion and celery. Cook until softened.

5. Cover with the carrot slices and place the chicken pieces on top of the carrots – legs and thighs at the bottom, breasts on top.

6. Season with salt and pepper. Add the elderflower, stock and lemon peel.

7. Bring to a simmer and cook gently for 40 minutes. The legs and thighs will braise and the breasts will steam, in effect.

8. Pour off the liquid into another pan and reduce over a high heat until it's to your liking. Sharpen with a little lemon juice.

Spiced-up Grilled Quail with Lentil Salad

The quail is a small, harmless bird with an endearing, gentle flavour. So why bother to eat it? Well, jollied up a bit, it makes a more than acceptable mouthful, it's quick and easy to cook, and it's best eaten in the fingers. And eating in the fingers encourages friendship and ease.

12 quail
3 lemons
olive oil
3 red chillies (medium hot)
salt and pepper
fresh thyme

1. Spatchcock the quails by cutting down the breastbone with a pair of scissors. Flatten them. Sprinkle them with the juice of 2 lemons and dribble some olive oil over them.

2. Finely chop the chilli.

3. Sprinkle the quails with the chopped chilli, salt and freshly ground pepper, and keep in a cool place for about an hour.

4. Pop under the grill breast-side down, not too close to the flame. You need to cook them through without incinerating them.

5. After 4 minutes turn them over and grill for another 4 minutes. They should be well tanned but not burned or leathery. Turn off the heat.

6. Strip the leaves off the thyme and scatter them over the resting birds. Let them rest for 5 minutes. Serve in a great pile on a plate in the middle of the table.

Lentil Salad

The secret of this salad is to use lots and lots of parsley and proportionately few lentils.

1 huge bunch of flat-leaf parsley
6dsp cooked lentils (see Chapter 3)
lemon juice
extra-virgin olive oil
salt and pepper

1. Chop the parsley somewhere between very fine and roughly.

2. Put in a bowl and add the lentils, mixing thoroughly.

3. Season with the lemon juice, olive oil, and salt and pepper.

Grilled Pork Chops

For years I had this vision of a grilled pork chop, tanned but tender and tasty, with a crest of crisp, golden fat running round its rim. I tried grilling them fast, I tried grilling them slow, over charcoal and under flame. Nothing seemed to make much difference. They always turned tight and tough and distinctly unbiddable. So I consulted some of the greatest minds in the country on the subject, and the greatest minds suggested brining the chops first. So I did and, well, oh my gosh, here was the perfect grilled pork chop, tanned and tender and tasty to the very last shred gnawed from the bone. You may think it's a lot of trouble to go to for a grilled pork chop. So it may be, but every now and then, when nothing else will do, just give it a go. And of course, you can do it for more than just two.

To brine the chops
3 litres water
150ml salt
75ml sugar
1 tsp peppercorns
1 tsp juniper berries
½ tsp allspice berries
4 bay leaves
6 pork chops

1. Bring all the ingredients to the boil.

2. Boil for 5 minutes. Skim, then cool.

3. Put the chops into a non-reactive dish.

4. Pour the brine over them and leave for 12 hours.

Grilling
6 brined chops
6 sage leaves
pepper

1. Pat the chops dry. Cut through the rind at regular intervals – every 2cm – so that it doesn't tighten and curl up during the grilling.

2. Turn on the grill to a high heat and slip the chops under. Leave for 4 minutes, then turn over and grill for a further 4 minutes.

3. Season with pepper and sprinkle with chopped sage leaves. Leave to rest for 8 minutes. Serve.

This is not a Fort original. I have lifted it straight from Elizabeth David. With no apology. In my crusade to persuade people to turn from the (expensive) primary cuts of meat to the less-favoured (and so cheaper) but frequently tastier cuts, I will turn for help wherever I can find it. And if we eat these less-favoured (and so cheaper) and tastier cuts, we will be wasting less of the unfortunate beast that has been slaughtered for our pleasure.

2 breasts of lamb
1 onion
2 carrots
1 stick of celery
1tsp black peppercorns
2 bay leaves
100g (roughly) Dijon mustard
6tbsp breadcrumbs

1. Turn on the oven to 170°C/325°F/Gas 3.

2. Place the breasts of lamb in a casserole along with the vegetables, peppercorns and bay leaves. Put it into the oven for 2½ to 3 hours.

3. Take the breasts out of the liquid and remove the bones (assuming they haven't been boned already). Allow to cool.

4. When you want to eat them, turn on the oven to 180°C/350°F/Gas 4.

5. Spread mustard all over – how much depends on how much you like mustard – and sprinkle with breadcrumbs.

6. Pop into the oven for 20 minutes and then slide under the grill until the breadcrumb crust goes golden and crunchy. Cut up and serve.

More finger food, and desperately untidy to eat. Never mind. Think of the fun. Think of the pleasure. Once you've grasped the principle (which, let's face it, isn't difficult), you can make up your own fillings. It's a nifty way of dressing up leftovers, too.

600g chicken
1 large onion
4 sticks celery
2 medium carrots
3 cloves garlic
2tbsp chopped fresh ginger
2tbsp vegetable oil
600g pork sausage meat
rice-wine vinegar
mirin
24 lettuce leaves (or more if you're hungry)
16 basil leaves

1. Dice the chicken pretty finely.

2. Chop the vegetables, garlic and ginger finely.

3. In a wok or frying pan heat the oil until it is smoking.

4. Add the pork and chicken, and fry until nice and brown.

5. Add the vegetables and the ginger and continue to cook until the onion is translucent. It you have cut the other vegetables small enough, they will cook in the same amount of time. If they are still a bit crunchy at the end, no matter.

6. Sprinkle with mirin and then with rice vinegar.
   Cook a little longer.

7. Scrape into a warm serving dish. Tear or chop the basil leaves and mix in.

8. Divide up the lettuce leaves. Plop a spoonful of the mixture into a lettuce leaf, fold the sides in to enclose it, and force it into your mouth.

Sweet and Sour Roasted Onions

I like recipes in which the cooking does all the work, as it were, and I can just muck about. This is very nice with grilled pork chops or the chicken wings above.

2 large onions
50ml olive oil
salt and pepper
2tbsp red wine
2tbsp red-wine vinegar
1dsp caster sugar
1 sprig thyme

1. Turn on the oven to 190°C/375°F/Gas 5.

2. Peel the outer skins from the onions, cut them in half and place them cut-side down in a roasting tray.

3. Pour the olive oil over them. Season with salt and pepper.

4. Cover with foil and bake in the oven for about an hour until they are soft. The onions should be soft but keep their shape.

5. At the end of the hour, pour off the oil and pour on the red wine, red-wine vinegar and the sugar.

6. Return to the oven uncovered and bake for a little longer

until most, but not all, of the liquid has evaporated.

7. Pull the leaves off the sprig of thyme and fling all over
    the onions.

Gooseberry and Elderflower Pie

Gooseberries and elderflower are an even more divine marriage
than chicken and elderflower (not to mention Astaire & Rogers,
Rodgers & Hammerstein or Rogers & Grey). And the whole
notion of pies wings me back to my childhood, when all the
world was safe and happy. Must have custard.

300g plain flour
125g butter, well chilled
½ tsp salt
cold water
1kg gooseberries
250g caster sugar
4tbsp elderfower syrup
beaten egg and water to glaze

1. Put the flour into a bowl. Grate the butter into the flour –
    it helps distribute the butter more evenly through the flour.

2. Add the salt and then enough water to make a good firm
    dough. Work the ingredients just enough to make everything
    nice and smooth and silky.

3. Turn on the oven to 220°C/425°F/Gas 7.

4. Divide the dough in half and roll it out as thinly as possible.
    Drape it over a well-buttered shallow pie dish. I use one of
    those metal ones with a removable base through which I
    have banged holes with a large nail so that the heat can

penetrate from underneath and so cook the pastry base at the same time as cooking the top. This is called a technological breakthrough. Let the lined dough rest for at least 1 hour.

5. Top and tail the gooseberries.

6. Cover the pastry base with them. Sprinkle with sugar and elderflower syrup.

7. Roll out the other half of the pastry as thinly as the bottom.

8. With your finger, dampen the edge of the lower pastry, where it drapes over the edge of the pie dish. Place the pastry top over the fruit and press the lid and the base together firmly all the way around, so they are well sealed.

9. Cut a few decorative slits in the top with the point of a sharp knife to let out the steam.

10. Paint the surface with the beaten egg and water to glaze it, then put it in the oven for 10 minutes before turning down the heat to 190°C/375°F/Gas 5 for further 30 minutes. Cool slightly before serving.

Nutella Ice Cream

My daughter, Lois, went through a period when all she wanted to eat, aside from pasta, was Nutella. And if I could have come up with a recipe for, say, farfalle with Nutella sauce, she would have been blessed out. You have to draw the line somewhere, and I drew it there. Still, I consoled her with Nutella ice cream. I found it quite consoling, too.

2 eggs
2tbsp caster sugar

1x284ml pot double cream
100ml milk
1 large pot of Nutella

1. Break the eggs into a deep bowl. Add the sugar, then beat with an electric whisk for 1 minute until pale and frothy.

2. Add the cream and whisk for another 20 seconds.

3. Add the milk and whisk for 10 seconds.

4. Add the Nutella bit by bit. It is pretty solid, so it takes some dispersing.

5. When you have a nice smooth custard, pour it into the freezing bowl of your ice-cream machine and churn until set; or put it into a plastic container, and pop it into your freezer, remembering to give it a stir every twenty minutes or so until frozen.

❧ making an effort ❧

Paul Heathcote's Clear Chilled Tomato Juice with Basil

Another gift from another writer, but so easy is this recipe – it requires not cooking for a start – and so exquisite are the results that it should be brought to as wide an audience as possible. It is one of the wonders of summer. You don't need to serve very much of it to everybody.

1.5kg over-ripe tomatoes
50g basil, chopped
115g chervil, chopped
bunch of flat-leaf parsley, chopped

1 shallot, finely chopped
125ml white wine
salt and pepper
pinch of sugar (optional)
more basil, chervil or tarragon for garnish

1. Place the over-ripe tomatoes in a large bowl or pot.
    Add the herbs and shallots and white wine. Season.

2. With your hands, squeeze the tomatoes until they are
    all crushed.

3. Place a piece of muslin in a large bowl as a lining and tip the
    tomato mixture into it. Tie up the muslin into a bag. If you
    have a sufficiently cold room hang this overnight to catch
    the juices; otherwise sit in a colander and set over a bowl
    in the fridge.

4. Paul says strain again, but that's chef perfection for you.
    I'm not sure it's necessary.

5. Put any herbs or vegetables you decide to use in the bottom
    of the soup bowls, glasses, or whatever you want to serve it
    in, and carefully pour the chilled juice over them. Garnish.

Sea Trout with Champagne Sabayon Sauce

I sort of prefer sea trout to salmon, partly because I like fishing
for them (which, sadly, is not the same as catching them), but
also because I find their flesh more refined and more delicate.
And that requires a refined and delicate sauce. Hollandaise sauce
is a key ingredient of the Sabayon. You can find quite decent
ready-made hollandaise sauces these days, but for the real cooks
I've included the easy method way of making your own.

Sea Trout
1 sea trout
2tbsp salt

1. Make sure the fish has been properly cleaned and the gills taken out.

2. Put into a pan, cover with water and add the salt.

3. Bring to a simmering point and turn off. Leave until ready to use.

Hollandaise sauce
125g unsalted butter
3 egg yolks
1 tbsp lemon juice
1 tbsp water
½ tsp salt

1. Melt the butter in a sauce pan.

2. Whiz up egg yolks, lemon juice, water and salt in a blender or food processor.

3. Continue whizzing while you slowly pour in the melted butter.

Sabayon sauce
1 green tomato
1 ripe tomato
1 onion
55g butter
Juice of ½ lemon
150ml fish stock
2tbsp whipping cream
100ml champagne
100ml hollandaise sauce
3 good sprigs of thyme

1. Blanch, peel, deseed and chop the tomatoes finely. Chop the onion very finely.

2. In a saucepan melt half the butter. Add the onion, tomatoes, thyme and lemon juice. Stew until soft.

3. Add the fish stock, turn up the heat and boil to reduce the liquid to about a quarter.

4. Make the hollandaise (3 egg yolks, 200g butter, juice of ½ lemon: melt the butter, put the egg yolks in a blender or food processor with the lemon juice. Pour in the melted butter as the blades are whirring.)

5. Whisk the whipping cream to just short of stiff.

6. Blend the champagne into the sauce base, the hollandaise into that and the whipped cream into the whole.

7. Reheat gently.

Chicken Sausage with Pistachios

I have to include this recipe. I've been doing it for years in various forms. The original inspiration was a recipe in A Taste of Italy by Giuliano Bugialli, and it is still recognisably his in spite of my tinkering. One of the major changes is that he suggests skinning the chicken to start with and then using the skin as the casing for the sausage. It's a bit of trouble, but not that much. However, in my experience most people discard the skin, so this just gives them the rest to eat.

1kg chicken meat (e.g. breast and thighs and/or 2 legs)
70ml double cream
salt and pepper
30g shelled pistachios
8-10 slices of prosciutto or other cured ham

1. Take the skin off all the chicken meat.

2. Put half the breast and both legs into a food processor and whizz until smooth.

3. Transfer to a bowl and fold in the cream. Season with salt and pepper – go carefully with the salt because the cured ham can also be quite salty.

4. Chop the other breast and the 2 thighs quite roughly and add to the chicken and cream glop.

5. Add the pistachios. Mix very thoroughly to make sure all the elements are evenly distributed. Chill for an hour.

6. On a large piece of kitchen foil lay out the slices of prosciutto or cured ham to form a rectangle roughly 20cm long by 12cm wide.

7. Place the chicken mix along the middle and then carefully fold the ham round the filling to form a sausage.

8. Wrap the foil around the sausage to reinforce the shape, folding the 2 edges together to seal it. Chill for 30 minutes.

9. While the sausages are chilling, turn on the oven to 190°C/375°F/Gas 5.

10. Put the foil-wrapped sausages on an oven tray and pop in for 45 minutes. Take out and remove the foil, being careful to keep any juices that have leached out of the meat.

11. Put the sausage back in the oven for another 10 minutes to crisp up the outside.

12. Serve with the juices you have kept, thickened with a little butter, or with chicken stock you have made earlier.

Slow Roast Rib of Beef

This will be a problem recipe for many people because it asks you to jettison everything you've been practising for years. It also means you may have to buy another piece of kitchen technology. But once you have done so, you will be liberated. No more abstruse calculations about how many minutes at which temperature. No more hit and miss. No more, 'I'm so sorry. I seem to have overcooked the beef. Again.' Or, 'What do you mean, you don't like it raw?'

The secret lies in the meat thermometer. The ideal internal temperature for beef is 52-54°C in my view. That will make it pink but not bloody, tender but not jelly-like, and tasty as that piece of beef will ever be. I have banged on about the whys and wherefores for this so often that I will pass on this occasion. Just take my word. It works.

The breed and provenance have parts to play. The butchery and hanging have parts to play (in an ideal world beef should be hung for 21 days). But the cooking has the biggest part to play if you want to get the best out of your beef.

You see, when you apply heat to a piece of meat, it causes the fibres to contract. This squeezes the meat's natural juices from the inside to the outside where they are caramelised in what is known as the Maillard reaction. The more juice you can keep inside the meat, the more succulent, tender and tasty it will be. That's why you always rest meat after roasting, so the juices that haven't been caramelised can flow back to where they came from.

By cooking your meat at a very low temperature, you will minimise the shrinking effect, and so the loss of juices and the loss of flavour, because it keeps virtually all the juices trapped inside the meat. This may all sound rather scientific, which of course it is (and just about the only bit of food science I have ever managed to absorb), but slow roasting is also the easiest way to cook it. In essence it means just bunging it in the oven and leaving it there until it gets to the right temperature. Of course, four people are unlikely to eat a whole rib on their own; but the next day you can have a thin slice of cold roast beef on a slice of bread spread with horseradish sauce, or a couple of slices with a baked potato sodden with dripping.

1 rib of beef on the bone (about 1.5kg)
salt and pepper

1. Turn on the oven to the lowest setting possible. It should be about 75°C/150°F.

2. Place the rib flat in a roasting tray or cast-iron pan and put it in the oven. Pour in a little water. Leave it there for 4 hours.

3. Test the temperature with your probe after 2½ hours. If the internal temperature is getting too close to the magic 52-54°C for comfort, turn the oven off for a while and let it cool. If it seems that it isn't getting warm enough, turn up the heat just a fraction. Test again in an hour.

4. When the rib has hit the temperature, or is within spitting distance of it, take it out of the oven.

5. Pour off the water together with any juices that might have oozed out into a saucepan.

6. The rib will look pretty unprepossessing at this point. You can easily handle it with your bare hands. Do not despair.

7. You can either turn up the oven to full blast for 10 minutes to let the heat really build up, putting the rib back into this seriously hot oven to brown up on the outside. Or you can put a little fat into a frying pan big enough to hold it side down, and brown on top for a couple of minutes on either side.

8. Either way, you end up with a piece of meat that has the majestic appearance of the traditionally roasted rib.

9. Let it rest in a warm place for 40 minutes or so. Season with salt and pepper on both sides just before carving.

10. I prefer to carve it by cutting the whole piece of meat off the bone and then carving it in thickish slices across the grain. That way everyone should get a proportion of creamy-amber fat to slice of meat, and the meat is easier to cut on the plate.

Shallot and Red Wine Sauce

A little sauce to lubricate the beef.

6 shallots
50g unsalted butter
200ml red wine
300ml beef stock
1dsp French mustard

1. Finely chop the shallots.

2. Melt half the butter in a saucepan. Add the shallots and cook until soft.

3. Add the wine and boil to reduce down to a tablespoonful.

4. Add the beef stock and reduce to about 140ml.

5. Stir in the mustard and then beat in the rest of the butter.

Pigeons can be something of a challenge for the home cook. They are cheap. They are plentiful, but if you're not careful, they can easily take on the resilience of a tennis ball. I still have painful memories of seeing one such culinary masterpiece skidding off the plate as a friend attempted to get his fork into it, and bouncing round the room. By coming at them this way, you should overcome its bouncing tendencies.

150g smoked bacon
5 carrots
5 sticks celery
55g butter plus 30g butter
2tbsp vegetable oil
6 wood pigeons
150ml white wine
chicken stock
salt and pepper
16-20 pickling onions
20-24 button mushrooms
170ml sour cream
1tbsp juniper berries
1tsp paprika

1. Cut one stick of celery and one carrot into quarters. Cut the bacon into sticks about 5mm wide.

2. Heat the 55g butter and 2tbsp oil in a casserole until foaming. Brown the pigeons.

3. Pour off the butter/oil when the pigeons are nicely tanned.

4. Add the bacon sticks and fry until their fat runs.

5. Add the quartered celery and carrot, then add the white wine and juniper berries and then enough stock to cover. Season

with salt and pepper.

6. Pop on the lid, lower the heat and simmer gently for 45 minutes to 1 hour. The flesh should get to the point where it is falling off the bone.

7. Cut the remaining carrots and celery into more sticks.

8. Heat 30g butter plus a little vegetable oil in a wide-bottomed pan. Add the onions and brown lightly. Then add the mushrooms and brown slightly.

9. Add the celery and carrots sticks and stir round. Leave off the heat.

10. When the pigeons are cooked, pour the cooking juices into the pan with the vegetables, paprika and the sour cream.

11. Place the pan over a high heat to reduce the juices and cook the vegetables – for about 10 to 15 minutes or when you find the whole kit and caboodle to your taste.

12. Pour over the pigeons.

Chicken Breasts in Almond and Lemon Sauce

Normally I am loath to cook just a breast, or just a leg or thigh come to that. I like to cook the whole bird, but every now and then you have to give way in the interests of portion control and eye appeal. I happen to think this dish tastes as good as it looks, if not better. The people to whom I served it thought so too, luckily for me.

6 chicken breasts, skins removed
120g leeks

2 shallots
25g butter
1 lemon
75ml white wine
100ml chicken stock
100ml double cream
80g ground almonds
salt and pepper

For stuffing the chicken breasts
250g spinach
100g onion
100g prosciutto
40g butter
salt and pepper

1. To make the stuffing: Chop the onions and prosciutto for the
    stuffing very fine indeed. Melt half the butter in a pan. Add
    the onions, prosciutto and spinach and fry gently until soft
    without browning them. Season.

2. With a sharp knife, slice the chicken down its length so that
    it opens like a pocket. Spread the stuffing inside each and
    then close it up again.

3. Wash the leeks finely and slice thinly. Chop the shallots finely.

4. Heat the rest of the butter in a deep frying pan or a sauté
    pan large enough to hold the chicken breasts. Add the leek
    and shallots and fry gently to soften without browning for
    10 minutes.

5. Add the juice of the lemon, keeping the peel. Add the
    vermouth (or white wine), stock and cream and simmer
    for 10 minutes.

6. Place the chicken breasts into the pan and simmer for

a further 10 to 12 minutes. Then take out the chicken breasts and keep warm.

7. Whizz the vegetable and liquid contents of the pan in a liquidiser until smooth.

8. Add the ground almonds and grate the lemon peel in as well. Season, then reheat the sauce until it thickens.

9. Serve over or under the chicken breasts, according to your fancy.

Sautéed-Casseroled Pork Chops

My love affair with the pork chop (continued).

6 pork chops
2tbsp pork or duck fat or vegetable oil
1 bunch thyme
3 cloves garlic
150ml white wine or vermouth or white port
1tbsp Dijon mustard (optional)
salt and pepper

1. Turn on the oven to 140°C/275°F/Gas1.

2. Heat the fat or oil in a frying pan until smoking. Put in the chops and brown on either side. This should take 2 or 3 minutes on each. You may have to do the chops in batches.

3. Season the chops when they have finished browning and transfer them to a casserole into which you have already put the bunch of thyme. Add the garlic.

4. Place the casserole over the heat until it begins to sizzle, then move it down to the oven. Leave for 15 minutes.

5. Check the temperature of a couple of the chops. They should be 65°C/150°F or a little above. If they aren't, turn up the oven to 150°C/300°F/Gas 2 and leave for another 5 minutes or so. Take out the chops and keep warm. Put the casserole over a high heat on the hob and add the white wine, vermouth or white port.

6. Boil away for 1 minute, scraping up the gooey bits on the bottom of the pan.

7. Mash in the garlic and stir in the mustard if you are using it. When you serve the chops, pour the juices over them.

Consomme de Vin au Fruits

Another by-product of disaster. I have only ever given one cookery lesson in public, for very good reasons. I had been extolling the virtues of wine jellies, set about with fruits of whichever season. When I went to demonstrate how to turn out that particular jelly, and carve it for mega plate effect, it hadn't set properly, and all the blobs of semi-set jelly wobbled off all over the work surface. I stared at it. My students stared at me. Then I remembered my own advice at the beginning – don't worry about disaster. Only you know what a dish is supposed to be before it graduates to the table. If things don't quite turn out the way you expected, change the title of the dish. Rapidly I scraped all the jelly back into a bowl and called for a soup plate. I sliced up some fruit, along with a few basil leaves and put them into the plate. I plopped some of the semi-set jelly on top. 'There,' I said. 'Consomme de Vin au Fruits d'Ete.' It was summer at the time. And actually, so damn delicious was it, it's been in the repertoire ever since.

1x75cl bottle of the cheapest sweet white wine
– Spanish moscatels do very nicely, as does a grapey Asti
1tsp gelatine

fruit – a selection/mixture of strawberries, nectarines, peaches, pears,
blackberries, blueberries
16 basil leaves

1. Pour the wine into a saucepan and bring to a gentle heat.
    It shouldn't get too hot or it will lose some of its flavour,
    but it must be hot enough to dissolve the gelatine.

2. Add the gelatine and stir to dissolve.

3. Pour the mixture into a bowl and set aside in a cool place
    to set.

4. Some time before you need to serve, peel and slice the
    nectarines/peaches/pears and divide up the slices and other
    fruit among the plates.

5. Slice the basil leaves into thin strips and scatter over the
    top. Stir the jelly to break it up and then divide up among
    the plates.

Pear and Quince Brioche Charlotte

A charlotte is so much lighter, more satisfying and sophisticated
than tarte tatins, I can't think why anyone bothers with the
latter. (All right, yes I do, but you know what I mean.) Normally
you'd make a charlotte with ordinary sliced white, but try brioche
by way of a change.

1kg Conference pears and quinces
2tbsp demerara sugar
100ml calvados (optional)
10 slices of brioche
150g unsalted butter
1dsp caster sugar

1. Turn on the oven to 200°C/400°F/Gas 6.

2. Peel and core the pears and quinces.

3. Put them into a saucepan with the demerara sugar and calvados if you are using it. Cover and cook over a gentle heat until the flesh has turned to pulp.

4. Take off the lid and continue cooking until the pear/quince pulp is medium solid. Allow to cool.

5. Melt the butter. Take a slice of the brioche and lay it down in the melted butter, one side only. Place the slice of brioche in the charlotte mould, buttered-side outwards. Repeat this with the other slices, keeping two aside for the top. If you need more butter, just melt it.

6. Once you have made the brioche box, as it were, fill up with the pear and quince mixture.

7. Place the remaining slices on top and sprinkle with the caster sugar. Pop into the oven for 15 to 20 minutes. Brioche bronzes (and burns) more quickly than bread. Serve with cream – why not?

6. figures of eight

Cooking, like politics, is about the art of the possible. Cooking for eight people is more than just an up-grade of cooking for six. You might just about consider cooking for six during the week, but eight is a different matter. Eight requires planning, shopping, effort and washing up, all of which are a lot to ask on top of eight hours in the office, plus an hour or so travelling either way. So not many people are likely to be cooking for large numbers during the week. Even I don't, and I'm a chap who likes to cook every day.

So this is for the weekends, when you've got time and inclination to shop and potter and spend some time about it. You can't rush cooking for eight. Even with all the modern cooking aid known to man, there's bound to be a good deal of preparation, sourcing, sorting, chopping, washing, etc., etc. On the other hand, you can make things easier on yourself by thinking things through thoroughly beforehand, planning things out, writing them down if necessary. And be sensible. Ambition's all very well in its way, but there's no need to apply it to every course. What you don't need is to have to finish three dishes, say, at the last minute. If you can have one or even two sorted earlier in the day or even the day before, you'll enjoy yourself a good deal more. And insert a cheese course before the pudding so that your guests can be tucking into that while you get stuck into the pudding.

And if things get out of hand, just drop a vegetable, or even a course if necessary. Panic communicates itself to guests just as much as it does to small children, with much the same effect. After all, cooking, and eating are supposed to be about pleasure, not suffering, or so I have come to believe. It wasn't always so, I must admit. There were times when things didn't turn out quite as I had hoped – the sea trout stuffed with herb soufflé episode springs to mind; I hadn't noticed that the sea trout were quite raw owing to an unnoticed oven malfunction until Stevie said, 'I thought something wasn't quite right when it winked up at me from the plate' – and I wanted to commit suppuru with one of my kitchen knives. And it took me a long time to be able to jettison a fancy effect if I was running out of time. Now I give it no mind. Just so long as the rest turns out all right.

✒ a piece of cake ✒

Potato Soup with Garlic

It started off in Italy, as so many of my ideas do. It seemed so simple, so delicious. And it was just potatoes, their cooking water, a little butter and seasoning. The original was served with crisp, fried octopus tentacles. Not easy to come by in Britain. But the garlic works wonders.

750kg potatoes (preferably new)
25g butter
4 cloves garlic
extra-virgin olive oil
salt and pepper

1. Clean the potatoes thoroughly but don't peel them.

2. Put them into a pan and cover with water.

3. Bring to the boil and cook until cooked i.e. you can stick a fork in quite easily. Strain off the cooking water and keep it.

4. Let the potatoes cool slightly and peel.

5. Put them through a potato ricer or mouli and then through a sieve back into the saucepan in which they were boiled.

6. Dilute with the potatoes' cooking water until you have the texture of single cream. Beat in the butter. Season.

7. Peel and finely slice the garlic cloves and fry in the olive oil until light brown and crisp.

8. Fling the cloves about on top of the soup and dribble a little more oil on top.

Adam Gebel's Chlwodnik

Adam Gebel, a.k.a. Adam the Pole, was married to my godmother, Pamela. He was a notable fisherman, cook, drinker and vigorous conversationalist. I lost count of the times bottles of iced vodka washed down pickled herring or pirogi, followed by bigos or what he called gwumky. Happy and halcyon dinners, they were. Anyway, in summer he liked to make this soup, refreshingly lactic and typically filling, with a wonderful Day-Glo pink from the beetroot.

2x285ml pots of buttermilk
1x285ml pot of smetana
4 hard-boiled eggs

1 cucumber
1 bunch of radishes
1 cooked beetroot
1 tbsp fresh dill

1. Mix the buttermilk and smetana in a bowl.

2. Slice the hard-boiled eggs and stir in.

3. Peel, deseed and dice the cucumber into small cubes and stir in. Wash the radishes, slice thinly and stir in.

4. Peel and cut the beetroot into small cubes and stir in.

5. Add the dill and stir in. Leave to meditate for at least 12 hours in the fridge. Eat cool.

Red Onion and Parma Ham Rolls

More of a nibble than a dish, although they would stack up nicely as a light first course.

8 red onions
olive oil
balsamic vinegar
12 slices of Parma (or other cured) ham
Parmesan

1. Peel and slice up the onions quite thickly.

2. Heat some oil in a frying pan and gently fry the onion until soft.

3. Cut all the slices of ham in half.

4. Lay some of the onion in the middle of one half, dab with balsamic vinegar and roll up like a carpet. Remember you have to do 24 of these, so measure out carefully.

5. Put the ham and onion rolls on a nonstick oven tray.

6. 5 minutes before serving pop them into the oven, pre-heated to 180°C/350°F/Gas 4.

7. Take them out when the ham has gone all crunchy – 3 or 4 minutes. Splash a little olive oil onto the centre of each serving plate. Place an onion and ham roll on the oil, put a sliver of Parmesan on each and get to the table.

Rabbit, Carrot and Celery Salad

I am very fond of rabbit, which is as cheap as it is versatile – three quid per rabbit at one of my local butchers. The saddle and back legs get the fancy treatment, but I have a tender spot for the front legs. There's not much meat on them, for sure, but they still have their place in the scheme of things, and they give a refined, sweet flavour to a crunchy salad.

8 rabbit front legs
500ml chicken stock
bunch of thyme plus 2 bay leaves
1 head of celery
3 carrots
juice of 1 orange
juice of ¼ lemon
3tbsp walnut/hazelnut/olive oil
salt and pepper

The rabbit legs
1. Turn on the oven to 150°C/300°F/Gas 2.

2. Place the legs in a casserole on top of the herbs. Cover with stock. Pop into the oven and leave there for at least 6 hours (or overnight or all day) until the meat is falling off the bone.

3. Take out the legs and discard the herbs.

4. Pull the meat off the bones, shred roughly, season with salt and pepper and keep until you're ready to finish off the salad. Allow to cool.

5. Boil down the cooking juices until you have 3-4tbsp left.

The celery salad
1. Break off all the stalks, and wash thoroughly. Keep the leaves.

2. With a very sharp knife, cut each stalk into matchsticks approximately 8cm long by 5mm wide. Put into ice-cold water and leave for at least an hour.

3. Do the same with the carrot. Chop the celery leaves.

Alternatively you can use one of those ingenious devices that looks like a peeler with sharp teeth to shred the celery and carrot. I have even used an ordinary peeler on occasion to produce ribbons, although this is quite labour intensive for 8 portions.

The dressing
1. Whisk together the rabbit juices, the orange and lemon juices and the oil to form an emulsion if you can. If you can't, not to worry.

Assembling the salad
1. Drain and dry the celery and carrot matchsticks (or ribbons). Place a heap in the middle of each plate.

2. Scatter the rabbit shreds over each.

3. Whisk the dressing one more time and pour a little over each. Scatter the chopped leaves over all. Very pretty.

Sausages with Beer and Onion Gravy

The perfect pork sausage – I have been searching for some such for half a lifetime, ever since Fort sausage supplier by family acclaim, Franklins the Butchers of Twyford, Berks, closed their doors for the last time, and their peerless plain pork bangers were no more. Recently I've tried my hand at making my own sausages (see page 225), but I regard this as a project in progress rather than a triumphant achievement. I tend to eat them on their own, but for a blob of tomato ketchup. But every now and then I want to dress them up a bit. Onion gravy is the classic gloop to put with them. I livened up the usual mixture with a dash of beer that I happened to be drinking at the time, Coniston Bluebird, and so liked the result I decided to write a recipe about it.

24-32 pork sausages
12 medium-sized white onions
50g pork fat/duck fat/ butter
1 litre light beer (Coniston Bluebird; Fuller's Honey Dew; Young's Waggledance)
1 star anise
1 bunch of thyme
salt and pepper

1. Gently fry the sausages in a pan (or roast them if you must in a 150°C/300°F/Gas 2 oven for at least 40 minutes.

2. Peel and slice the onions finely.

3. Melt the fat or butter in a casserole.

4. When it is smoking toss in the onions and fry until beginning to soften.

5. Pour in the beer and add the star anise.

6. Simmer for 50 to 60 minutes.

7. The liquid should have reduced by now and you should have a wonderful kind of oniony, beery glop. Stick the thyme into it and let that sit for 5 minutes or so to infuse.

8. Remove the thyme. Season. Serve.

Lamb and Sheep's Cheese Rissoles

Supper number. A fine way of using up leftovers.

1kg cooked lamb
350g sheep's cheese
1 onion
3 sprigs of rosemary
6tbsp breadcrumbs
2 eggs
salt and pepper
6tbsp olive oil

1. Mince the lamb or whizz it up in the blender. Grate the cheese. Chop up the onion finely. Pull the rosemary leaves off the stalks and chop quite finely.

2. Heat 2tbsp of olive oil in a frying pan.

3. Over a moderate heat fry the chopped onion until translucent – about 5 minutes.

4. Decant into a bowl, along with the minced lamb, cheese, rosemary and 2tbsp of breadcrumbs. Season.

5. Add the eggs and mix thoroughly.

6. Carefully mould the mixture into whatever shape and size you think rissoles should be. Roll them in the remaining breadcrumbs.

7. Heat the remaining oil in a frying pan and fry gently until brown and crunchy on the outside. Very nice with tomato sauce.

Cider Potatoes

To go with most meat dishes.

6 large baking potatoes
(e.g. Cara, Golden Wonder, Maris Piper, Romano)
1 litre sweet cider (or apple juice)
50g butter
pinch of salt

1. Peel the potatoes and cut them into 2.5cm slices.

2. Use a 5cm pastry cutter to cut the slices into rounds.

3. Put the potato slices into a large pan. Cover with the cider or apple juice. Add the butter and salt.

4. Place the pan over a high heat and bring to the boil. Reduce the liquid until it is syrupy and caramelisation has begun.

5. Turn the potatoes and gently colour them until they are coloured on both sides.

6. If the potatoes are coloured but not cooked, add a little water and repeat the process. Remove and keep warm.

OK, so it's not good for the heart, but it is for the soul, and I'm not suggesting you eat it ever day.

500g blackberries
55g caster sugar
2tbsp crème de mure or crème de cassis
juice of ¼ lemon
1 lardy cake

1. Place all the ingredients except for the lardy cake and the lemon juice in a saucepan and heat gently until the blackberries begin to ooze their juices and the sugar has dissolved. Taste.

2. Add lemon to help bring out the flavour of the fruit. Add a little more sugar if you think it needs it.

3. Cut the lardy cake into 8 decent slices and grill until it's warm and squidgy.

4. To the plate with it and plop the blackberries on top of each.

5. Serving suggestion: clotted cream.

no sweat

Another product of my attempts one year to keep pace with the over-production of sorrel and cucumbers. Nicely refreshing on a hot day.

4 eggs
1 small onion
1 cucumber
50g butter
400g sorrel
600ml vegetable or chicken stock
285ml sour cream
salt and pepper

1. Hard-boil the eggs and cool under running water until cold.

2. Chop the onion finely. Peel and slice the cucumber.

3. Heat the butter in a saucepan until foaming. Add the
    onion. Fry gently for 5 minutes. Add the sorrel. Cook for
    30 seconds. Stir and add the cucumber, and the stock.
    Cook for 5 minutes.

4. Whizz the sorrel, cucumber and stock in a food processor
    or blender.

5. Add the sour cream and whizz briefly again.

6. Peel and chop the hard-boiled eggs. Add to the soup. Season.

7. Cool and then chill. Serve.

Roast Cod with Chickpea and Vegetable Stew and Pesto

I think you have to be a bit careful with pesto, whether you make
your own or buy it. According to Genovese folklore – pesto
comes from Liguria – it should only be used to go with pasta,
preferably trenette. But it is v. useful for giving a bit of spirit to
other combinations, like this one.

200g dried chickpeas
4 medium carrots
1 small swede
1 turnip
2 onions
2 cloves garlic
extra-virgin olive oil
115ml chicken or vegetable stock
8 good person-sized chunks of cod fillet
salt and pepper
8dsp pesto

1. Soak the chickpeas overnight. Bring to the boil in fresh water and cook until soft. This should take about 40 to 60 minutes. Drain. (Alternatively, drain 2 tins of ready-cooked chickpeas.)

2. Chop up the carrots, swede and turnip until they are the equivalent size of the chickpeas. Chop the onions and garlic finely.

3. Heat the olive oil in a saucepan. When it goes all mazy, put in all the vegetables except the chickpeas.

4. Cook until the onion goes transparent. Add the chicken stock and the chickpeas. Season. Continue cooking until the vegetables are cooked through but not soggy.

5. Turn on oven to maximum.

6. Heat some oil in a roasting pan until smoking.

7. Put the cod fillets into it, sprinkle with coarse salt and pop into the oven for about 7 minutes. The fish should be just cooked through.

8. When it comes to serving, put a spoonful or two of vegetables on the plate. Swirl a desertspoonful of pesto into each and then plonk the cod on top.

Confit of Duck Legs

Another long and slow and nothing-much-for-the-cook-to-do job. You can cook these in batches and freeze them, if you like. They make a splendid stand-by for emergencies. You can fry some potatoes in the fat, too, or serve them with the cider potatoes above. Or lentils. Or a green salad, if you must.

8 duck legs
1 bunch of thyme
4 bay leaves
salt and pepper
150ml white wine
800g duck fat

1. Turn on the oven to 150°C/300°F/Gas 2.

2. Lay the thyme and bay leaves all over the base of the pan. Put the duck legs on top.

3. Pour in the white wine. Sprinkle the skins with salt and pepper (go very easy on the salt if you've brined them first). Scoop the duck fat onto the duck legs.

4. Slip the pan into the oven and leave for 3 hours. This should be enough time for most of the fat to melt out of the legs, leaving the meat tender and tasty right up to the end. You can do this all a few days before.

5. Keep the legs in their fat in the fridge until needed and reheat by frying them skin-side down until hot through. This will also give extra crispness to the skin.

Of beef, naturally. One of those old-fashioned, low-fat, rather rigorous cuts that blossom when looked after with tenderness and understanding i.e. cooked long and slow.

1 onion
1 carrot
2 celery stalks
olive oil
1.5kg brisket in the piece
1l red wine
150ml red-wine vinegar
whole head of garlic
2 bay leaves
1dsp juniper berries
1dsp black peppercorns
salt

1. Preheat the oven to 190°C/375°F/Gas 5.

2. Roughly chop the onion, carrot and celery. Heat 2tbsp oil in a casserole or roasting pan large enough to take the shoulder. Brown the vegetables in the hot fat – about 10 minutes.

3. Add the brisket, wine, vinegar, garlic, bay leaves, juniper berries and peppercorns.

4. Pop the lid of the casserole on or cover with 2 layers of foil and slide into the oven for 2 hours; 30 minutes before the end of cooking, take off the casserole lid or foil. This will have the effect of browning the top of the shoulder and reducing the bubbling liquid. At the end of the 2 hours, pour off this liquid into a saucepan, let it settle for 5 minutes or so, and then spoon off as much fat as you can.

5. While this is happening, excavate the head of garlic, squeeze

the soft flesh onto a plate and mash it up.

6. Taste the fat-free liquid, and if it isn't strong enough for your liking, boil it down until it is. Season with salt. Add the mashed garlic to it (or to the mashed potato, see below).

Potato Pie with Mozzarella, Prosciutto and Confit Tomatoes

I was trying to learn Italian at the time. In the course of one lesson, our teacher, the indefatigable Valeria, mentioned this dish. I was so entranced by it that I made detailed notes. If only I had been able to pay equal attention to the rest of her lessons. Of course you can vary the filling depending on what's available.

500g floury potatoes (eg. Cara, Golden Wonder, King Edward, Maris Piper, Pentland Crown)
175ml milk
2 eggs
115g grated Parmesan
salt and pepper
45g butter
2tbsp breadcrumbs

For the filling
150g mozzarella
150g prosciutto
150g confit tomatoes
2 dried red chillies

1. To confit the tomatoes: Turn on the oven to a low setting – 150°C/300°F/Gas 2. Slice the tomatoes in half. Splash some olive oil on a baking tray and arrange the tomatoes on it. Dribble some more oil over them and season with salt and pepper. Pop them into the oven and leave them there for 3 to 4 hours until they are semi-dried.

2. Turn up the oven to 190°C/375°F/Gas 5.

3. Wash the potatoes. Do not peel. Put them into a saucepan, cover with cold water and bring to the boil. Simmer until cooked, 20 to 30 minutes, depending on size and age.

4. Drain, cool and peel them while still warm. Mash or, even better, put through a food mill or potato ricer.

5. Heat the milk in a saucepan. Do not boil. As soon as little bubbles form around the edge, pour into the mashed potato. Beat in thoroughly.

6. Separate the eggs and beat the yolks on to the potato.

7. Add the butter and cheese and beat those in.

8. Whisk the egg whites until stiff, then fold them into the potato mixture. Butter the inside of an ovenproof dish such as a soufflé dish. Sprinkle 1tbsp of breadcrumbs all over the inside.

9. Plop half the potato mixture into the dish. Arrange the mozzarella, prosciutto and confit tomatoes on top, like the filling for a cake. Scoop the rest of the potato mixture on top.

10. Sprinkle the remaining breadcrumbs on top and slide into the oven until golden and crunchy on top – 20 to 25 minutes.

Mashed Potato

Cooking potatoes is one of the very few uses I can find for a microwave. It has the effect of steaming them within their own skins, so keeping all their flavour. However, the skin will be soft and flabby and if you want to eat them as baking potatoes, finish them of in a hot oven – 200°C/400°F/Gas 6 – for 5-10 minutes to harden up the outside. It's vital to turn them over every so often, or you will end up with a very odd hard lump on the bottom for some reason.

1kg floury potatoes (Cara, Pentland Squire, Maris Piper, Romano, King Edward)
150ml full-cream milk
85g unsalted butter
salt

1. Cook the potatoes at full power in the microwave until cooked, turning them over every 10 minutes so. This could take up to 25 minutes.

2. Peel and mash. I put mine through a potato ricer, which makes the flesh lighter and drier still.

3. Bring the milk to the boil and then beat into the riced potato. Cut the butter into smallish bits and beat them in, too. Season with salt to your taste.

Spiced Aubergine

The aubergine originated in India, where it grows wild. It migrated slowly westwards, growing larger all the time. Eventually it entered the Mediterranean mainstream from Turkey.

2 onions
50g fresh ginger
3 fresh red chillies
3 aubergines
4tbsp vegetable or olive oil
1tsp turmeric
1tsp ground cumin
1tsp ground coriander
½ tsp chilli powder

3tbsp red-wine vinegar
150ml tomato passata
salt and pepper

1. Peel and thinly slice the onions. Peel and finely dice the ginger. Chop up the chillies finely.

2. Cut the aubergines up into chunks about 2cm square. Sprinkle generously with salt and leave in a colander to exude liquid for 40 minutes or so. Rinse off the salt thoroughly and pat dry with kitchen towel.

3. Heat the oil with the chopped chilli in a frying pan or sauté pan and, when almost smoking, add the aubergines.

4. Fry the aubergines for 5 minutes or so, turning with a spatula.

5. Add the onions, turn down the heat and fry until softened – 5 to 8 minutes.

6. Add the spices one after the other, turning the aubergine and onion after each to make sure they are properly coated.

7. Add the ginger. Continue cooking for 10 minutes.

8. Turn up the heat, pour in the vinegar, bring to the boil.

9. Add the passata and turn down the heat until the aubergines are soft but not mushy. Season with salt and pepper.

Onion, Anchovy and Mozzarella Calzone

A kind of folded-over pizza, or pasty, I suppose you could call it. It's a good way to package food.

5tbsp salted capers
600g pizza dough
1kg red onions
16 anchovy fillets
800g mozzarella
salt and pepper
olive oil

1. Turn on the oven to 220°C/425°F/Gas 7.

2. Rinse the capers and soak in water for 30 minutes.

3. Divide the pizza dough into 8. Roll each out to make a circle
   about 15cm across.

4. Divide the other ingredients between them.

5. Moisten the edge of the dough with water, fold over, and
   squeeze the edges together to seal them. Fold the joined edge
   onto itself and squeeze down to make sure the seal is secure.

6. Brush with olive oil. Bake for 20 minutes until crisp and
   brown. Brush with oil again and serve.

Red and White Currant Pie

What can you do with red or white currants except make them
into jelly? My mother likes to leave them on their stalks and wash
them before dipping them in icing sugar. I like to make this pie.

For the pastry
500g plain flour
55g icing sugar
250g unsalted butter
75ml cold water
1 egg (for sealing later)

1. Put the flour and icing sugar into a bowl.

2. Grate the butter into it and then mix in with fingertips (or in your food processor).

3. Add the water little by little until you have a nice, firm dough.

4. Wrap in clingfilm and leave for 2 hours.

For the filling
125g redcurrants
125g white currants
2tbsp redcurrant jelly
250g caster sugar

1. Turn on the oven to 200°C/400°F/Gas 6.

2. Divide the pastry in half. Roll out one half. Butter the flan dish and line it with the rolled-out pastry, leaving a little overlapping the edge of the dish all the way round.

3. Fill with the currants, distributing them evenly. Sprinkle with the sugar and then plop the redcurrant jelly about.

4. Roll out the other half of the pastry. Beat the egg with a little water and then use it to paint the overlapping edge of the pastry in the dish. Put the second half of the pastry on top of the fruits to form a lid, pressing down all the way round where the two pastries meet to seal them.

5. Brush the lid of the pie with the rest of the egg and water. Make a few arrow cuts with the end of a sharp knife to let out the steam and bake for 25 to 30 minutes until golden.

Blackberry and Apple Clafouti

Blackberry and apple pie. Blackberry and apple crumble.
Blackberry and apple jelly. Why not blackberry and apple
clafouti? No reason.

For the batter
285ml milk
55g caster sugar
3 eggs
1tbsp vanilla essence
⅛ tsp salt
60g plain flour
grated zest of 1 lemon
butter

For the filling
450g apples (Bramley if you must, but better by far would be Reinette
d'Orleans, Bleinheim Orange, Lord Derby, Newton Wonder or, best
of all, Peasgood Nonsuch)
caster sugar
juice of ½ lemon
225g blackberries

1. Turn on the oven to 180°C/350°F/Gas 4.

2. Put all the batter ingredients into a food processor in the
   listed order. Whizz for a minute.

3. Peel, core and slice the apples, put them in a bowl with the
   lemon juice and sprinkle with sugar. Turn the slices over and
   over until they are coated with sugar and lemon juice.

4. Butter a baking dish and pour in enough batter to cover
   the bottom.

5. Pop into the oven for a couple of minutes or so to set
   the base.

6. Lay the slices of apple on top. Sprinkle the blackberries evenly about.

7. Pour in the rest of the batter.

8. Bake for about an hour. The clafouti should have puffed up and be nicely brown. Dust with icing sugar for artistic effect.

❧ making an effort ❧

Carpaccio of Smoked Haddock and Shredded Fennel with Orange Dressing

Think of this as the thoughtful person's smoked salmon, elegantly decked out. Smoked haddock lends itself to the carpaccio treatment marvellously well. It is naturally firm, and therefore easy to slice. It has what you might call a positive flavour. And you can carpaccio it earlier in the day. Just cover each plate with clingfilm. Uncover when you need to serve, and carry on with the rest of the assembly.

500g smoked, undyed haddock fillet
2 bulbs of fennel
1 orange
extra virgin olive oil
pepper

1. Very carefully cut slices off the fillet, angling the knife slightly downwards and cutting towards the tail. Cut as thinly as you can. It doesn't matter if some slices are bigger than others. Lay each slice onto the plates your guests will eat off. Just keep on slicing and dividing up until the fillet has all gone. Season with pepper.

2. Slice the fennel as thinly as possible (I use a cheap plastic mandolin).

3. Peel the orange, cutting away as much of the pith as possible. Cut out each segment from the surrounding membrane and then cut up into fine pieces.

4. Mix the orange with the fennel slivers, and divide up among the plates, piling it up in the middle.

5. A little dribble of olive oil and your work is done.

Soupe au Pistou

Pistou is the Nicoise version of pesto, a little less highly evolved perhaps, but very fine all the same. And it adds a blast of basil to the soup, which is pretty packed with summery stuff as it is.

Soup
225g dried haricot blanc beans (or 1x435g tin)
4 carrots
4 potatoes
4 leeks
225g French beans
2 bunches spring onions
90g broken vermicelli
bunch of thyme, rosemary and marjoram
pinch of saffron

Pistou
4 cloves mashed garlic
4tbsp tomato concentrate
4tbsp chopped fresh basil
55g grated Parmesan
extra virgin olive oil
salt and pepper

Soup

1. Soak the beans overnight. Place in a saucepan. Cover with plenty of cold water. Bring to the boil. Cook until soft.

2. Dice the onion, leek, carrots and potatoes, tail the green beans and cut in half.

3. Pour 2tbsp olive oil into a saucepan. Add the onion and leek. Fry until soft.

4. Add the carrots, potatoes, and 2 litres of water. Bring to the boil and simmer for 15 minutes. Add the vermicelli, spring onions, French beans and haricot beans and saffron, and simmer for another 15 minutes. Season. Plunge the herbs into the hot soup and leave to infuse for 10 minutes or so.

5. Dribble a little oil over the surface of the soup and it is ready for the pistou, which should be served separately in a bowl for people to help themselves to as much or as little as they fancy.

Pistou

1. In a food processor blitz the garlic, tomato concentrate, basil and Parmesan. Dribble in a little olive oil while the blades are still whirring. Keep on dribbling until you have a thick paste.

Saupiquet de Lapin

A.k.a. a French rabbit stew, packed to bursting point with juicy flavours. I once served it to a table that included the great Simon Hopkinson, the celebrated Rowley Leigh and the magisterial Alastair Little. Simon had the audacity to ask for mustard to go with his, and the rest followed suit. I still think they were wrong.

2 wild rabbits, cut into 8 pieces

For the marinade
140ml red-wine vinegar
2 onions, sliced
1 carrot, sliced
2 cloves garlic, sliced
2 sticks celery, sliced
1dsp juniper berries
1tsp black pepper corns
2 bay leaves
2 sprigs thyme
1 bunch parsley

For cooking
225g unsmoked bacon or pancetta
400g red onions
115ml olive oil
rabbit's liver
salt and pepper
3tbsp plain flour
1 bottle of beefy red wine
400ml rabbit, veal or beef stock
4 anchovy fillets
1 large bunch of thyme

1. Mix all the marinade ingredients together in a bowl large enough to hold the rabbit pieces as well. Marinade for at least 24 hours.

2. Slice the onions thinly and cut the bacon/pancetta into thick matchsticks.

3. Heat the olive oil in a frying pan. Fry the onions and bacon/pancetta until the onion is golden brown. Transfer them to a casserole.

4. Take the rabbit pieces out of the marinade and dry thoroughly with kitchen towel.

5. Brown the rabbit pieces, including the liver, in the frying pan before transferring them to the casserole. Season with salt and pepper and then dust with the flour, making sure that it is evenly distributed.

6. Heat the oven to 230°C/450°F/Gas 8.

7. Bring the casserole to sizzling point on the top of the cooker and transfer down to the oven, leaving it uncovered for 5 minutes.

8. Turn the rabbit pieces over and cook for another 5 minutes.

9. Strain the marinade and pour into the pan in which you have fried the onion, bacon and rabbits. Boil down until all you have is about a quarter left, scraping up all the gunge as you do so. Add the wine, and boil that down by half.

10. Add this liquid to the casserole, and then the stock, making sure everything is well mixed together.

11. Bring the casserole to simmering point on top of the stove, and let it putter away for about an hour until the rabbit is seriously tender.

12. Test the liquid. It should be thick enough to just coat the back of a spoon. If it is too runny, strain it off into a clean pan and boil until it has the right consistency.

13. Add the anchovy fillets and stir until they are dissolved. About 10 minutes before serving, push the sprig(s) of thyme into the sauce and let it rest there until you serve.

Turnips and pork have the kind of relationship that I have with dogs – warm, loving and mutually admiring. Pot roasting the pork all but eliminates the danger of it becoming dry and tough.

2.5kg loin of pork on the bone
2 cloves garlic
8 sage leaves
6tbsp pork fat or vegetable oil
1 onion
1 carrot
16 small or 6 large turnips
100ml white-wine vinegar
285ml white wine
salt and pepper

1. Turn on the oven to 150°C/300°F/Gas 2.

2. Remove the crackling from the loin carefully.
    Put to one side.

3. Cut down one side of the joint between the meat and
    the bone. It doesn't much matter which side.

4. Peel and slice the cloves of garlic very finely.

5. Arrange the garlic slices and the sage leaves along the face
    of the exposed meat, then tie the meat back to the bone.

6. Heat half the fat to smoking point in a frying pan and brown
    the joint all over.

7. Melt the remaining fat in a casserole.

8. Slice the onion and carrot finely and add. Fry gently for
    5 minutes.

9. Move the meat to the casserole. Cover and move down to the oven. Leave there for 2½ to 3 hours or until your trusty meat thermometer registers 185°F/55°C, basting the joint two or three times with its own juices as you go.

10. Bring a pot of salted water to the boil. Cut large turnips into quarters. Drop them or the small turnips into the boiling water and cook for 10 minutes. Take out. Drain and put into the casserole with the pork.

11. Take the pork and turnips out and keep warm.

12. Add the vinegar to the casserole and bring to the boil on a hob. Scrape up all the gunge stuck to the bottom.

13. Add the white wine. Mash the vegetables and boil until the juices have all reached the intensity that suits you. Remember that you need a fair amount to go round. You could pass the juices through a sieve at this point, but I wouldn't bother.

Slow Roast Loin of Mutton

I am a glutton for mutton. Of course you can use hogget (lamb between one and two years old; sheep has to be two or over to qualify as mutton) and even late lamb at a pinch, but there's nothing like the real McCoy to make this dish sing. Bully your butcher into tracking some down.

1 loin of mutton (bone in)
100ml vegetable oil
100g butter
150g each finely diced onion, garlic, leek, carrot, celery, fennel
100g shallots
1 bouquet of herbs (thyme, parsley, bay leaf, tarragon)

300ml beer (Timothy Taylor's Landlord or Innes & Gunn's Oak Aged)
300ml lamb or chicken stock

1. Heat the vegetable oil and butter in a roasting tray. Place the loin in it and fry until golden all over. Take the meat out of the roasting tray/casserole and keep warm.

2. Add the vegetables, and the herbs. Pour on the beer. Boil to reduce it by half.

3. Add the stock and bring to the boil.

4. Place the loin on the vegetables and cover with 2 layers of foil.

5. Preheat the oven to 150°C/300°F/Gas 2.

6. Roast in the oven for about an hour. Turn down the oven as low as possible, take off the foil and cook for a further 30 to 45 minutes, basting from time to time until the loin is beautifully glazed.

7. Remove the meat and pour off the liquor into another pan through a fine sieve.

8. Beat in a little butter. Season to taste and add some finely chopped tarragon and parsley.

Poached and Roasted Saddle of Venison

Another big dish for a big occasion. It looks good. It tastes good. By golly, it is good. Again, you'll have to find a butcher worthy of the name to get hold of a saddle, roe doe if he can manage, and you'll probably pay through the nose for it. But your friends will love you for it, and remember it for the rest of their lives, and that's what cooking is really about. Isn't it?

1 whole fillet of venison in the piece
100g unsmoked pancetta cut in thin slices
pepper

1. Turn on the oven to 220°C/425°F/Gas 7

2. Lay out a piece of clingfilm a bit longer than the fillet of venison. Place the venison on top. Cover the fillet with overlapping slices of pancetta. Wrap the clingfilm around them both to form a long sausage.

3. Put it into a casserole or pan of gently simmering water until the internal temperature of the meat reaches 50°C. If, like me, you sometimes misplace you digital meat thermometers, 30 minutes should be enough.

4. Take off the clingfilm cladding, transfer the fillet and pancetta to a roasting pan and give it a blast for 10 minutes.

5. Let it rest for 30 minutes in a warm oven until it is time to carve.

Chocolate and Chestnut Sauce

If you make this with the stock from the bones from your venison saddle, make the stock the day before. I just boiled the bones in water and then reduced it down until I got the concentration of flavour that I wanted. You could beef it up with pork (e.g. spare ribs) or unsmoked bacon or chicken bones or whatever. The chocolate might seem to be something of a novelty touch, but don't be afraid. It helps pull the sauce together and just adds a touch of smooth richness and a curious note to the sauce that will keep people chattering about it all night. Jane Grigson thought it was all right to put a chocolate sauce with hare, after all, and who am I to challenge that immaculate writer's judgement?

1 onion
1 stick of celery
1 medium carrot
55g unsalted butter
75ml brandy or Armagnac
150ml red wine
285ml stock
2 bay leaves
1 tbsp black peppercorns
150g peeled, cooked chestnuts
2 squares dark chocolate

1. Finely dice the vegetables.

2. Melt the butter in a saucepan. Add the diced vegetables and stew until soft.

3. Turn up the heat and add the brandy or Armagnac. Boil until there is hardly any left.

4. Pour in the red wine and do the same.

5. Add the bay leaves, peppercorns and stock. Cook over a fairly fierce heat for 20 minutes.

6. Strain into another pan. Reduce until you have quite an intense flavour, but remember you need a decent amount for 8 people.

7. Whizz all but 4 of the chestnuts in the food processor until pretty much pulverised. Add to the stock. Stir until the sauce has thickened up.

8. Just before serving, add the chocolate and stir until dissolved.

9. Roughly chop the remaining chestnuts and add to the sauce.

Steak and Kidney in Thyme-flavoured Pudding

I'm sure someone has thought of doing this before, but I can't find a reference to it. The thyme just lifts the suet jacket, as they say, and wafts a little herby breath all over the rich, rolling steak and kidney.

800g braising beef
2 onions
4 carrots
2 ox kidneys
2tbsp plain flour
1 bay leaf
4tbsp cider vinegar
150ml cider
150ml beef stock
salt and pepper

For the suet pastry
350g self-raising flour
175g shredded suet
1tsp of dried thyme or 1dsp fresh thyme leaves
salt and pepper
iced water

1. To make the suet pastry: Mix the flour, suet, thyme leaves, salt and pepper in a bowl and add enough water to make a good suet dough. Roll out three-quarters of it and line a 1.2-litre pudding basin with it so that some of the pastry just covers the lip of the basin.

2. Cut the beef into decent-sized chunks.

3. Peel and slice the onions and carrots, not too finely.

4. Cut up the ox kidneys similarly, taking care to cut out all fat and the gristly core.

5. Roll the beef in the flour and carefully place in the lined basin. Ditto the kidney.

6. Carefully tuck the onion and carrot pieces in around them. Tuck in the bay leaf.

7. Add the vinegar, cider and stock. Season with lots of pepper and a little salt.

8. Roll out the rest of the pastry to form a lid. Dampen the edges of the pastry lining the basin and place the lid on, pressing down to form a seal.

9. Cover with a double sheet of foil pleated in the middle so that it can expand while the boiling is going on. Tie the foil securely in place with string and lower the basin into a saucepan full of boiling water.

10. Boil for 5 hours, checking that the water hasn't boiled away in the meantime and topping up accordingly.

Aubergine, Potato and Feta Pie

I had this packet of filo pastry hanging around my fridge for weeks until I began to feel guilty about neglecting it. Then I noticed it was past its use-by date. I took it out, inspected it, sniffed it. There didn't seem to be anything wrong with it, so I set to there and then to put both it and me out of our misery, using up a few other bits and bobs that were getting near the end of their useful lives. It made a fine course at lunch that Saturday.

1kg aubergines
425g potatoes
250g onion

4 cloves garlic
1x500g packet of filo pastry
100g melted butter
400g feta cheese
1 egg
salt and pepper

1. Turn the oven on to 180°C/350°F/Gas 4.

2. Slice the potatoes very thinly and the aubergines quite thinly.

3. Blanch them both in boiling water, the potatoes very briefly, 30 seconds at most, the aubergines for a minute or two. Drain and dry carefully.

4. Peel and chop the garlic finely. Grate the onions.

5. Heat 2tbsp olive oil in a frying pan. Fry the garlic and onions gently.

6. Butter the base and inside of a tart dish. Working quickly and carefully, take the filo pastry out of its packet and line the dish with three or four leaves of pastry, painting each with butter before you lay the next on top.

7. Now fill the pastry case with a layer of aubergine slices and then a layer of potato slices, scattering some of the onion and garlic mixture and crumbling some of the feta on each, making sure it is quite even until all the filling is used up, seasoning as you go.

8. Lay 3 or 4 more layers on top, buttering each of them. Tuck the sides down so that the filling is completely enclosed. Beat the egg. Paint the edges of the pastry layers so they will form a seal. Paint the top of the pie with the remains of the beaten egg.

9. Bake for 25 to 35 minutes until golden brown. Turn out and eat hot or warm.

Creamy Onion Tart

A first course, really. And, by golly, it's creamy and yummy and generally rather delicious. So delicious, in fact, that I'm not sure that one will be enough. Better make two.

500g short-crust pastry (280g plain flour, 120g unsalted butter, 4tbsp iced water)
1kg white onions
115g butter
3 large eggs
285ml double cream
150g grated Gruyere
pepper
8 slices of prosciutto
115g grated Parmesan

1. Turn on the oven to 190°C/375°F/Gas 5.

2. Line a 23cm tart dish with the pastry, then line the pastry with greaseproof paper. Weight with baking weights and blind-bake for 35 to 45 minutes.

3. Peel and slice the onions thinly. Fry in the butter until soft and slightly golden. Keep to one side.

4. Pour the cream into a bowl. Break the eggs into it and beat in. Beat in the Gruyere. Mix thoroughly. Season with pepper.

5. Add the onions and mix again.

6. Line the part-baked base of the tart with the slices of prosciutto.

7. Fill with the onion/cream/Gruyere mix.

8. Sprinkle with the grated Parmesan and slip back into the oven for a further 25 minutes.

Ballotine of Savoy Cabbage with Swede and Chestnut

A showy vegetable construction for a pukka dinner party. Would go very nicely with the venison.

1 medium Savoy cabbage
1kg swede
500ml chicken stock
2 eggs
115g butter
salt and pepper
250g cooked peeled chestnuts
500ml stock

1. Cut away the outside leaves of the cabbage. Keep them (you will need 8 to 10 of them). Core and finely slice the rest.

2. Bring a pot of water to the boil. Blanch the outside leaves for 1 minute, lift out, plunge into cold water and drain.

3. Blanch the rest of the cabbage for 2 minutes, drain, plunge into cold water, and drain again.

4. Peel the swede and cut up into chunks. Cook in the chicken stock until soft – about 20 minutes. Drain.

5. Put the swede into the food processor with the butter and the egg and whizz until puréed. You can do with this swede because its high-fibre texture stops it from turning to glue, as potatoes do if you give them the food processor treatment. Season according to your taste.

6. Chop the chestnuts not too finely and mix into the swede purée.

7. Lay out a large piece of muslin (or drying-up cloth, or Jeye cloth), and lay out the blanched outer cabbage leaves so they form a largish rectangle, but within the larger rectangle of the muslin.

8. Smear the swede/chestnut purée all over the cabbage leaves, leaving it about 1.5cm short of the outer edge of the leaves.

9. Arrange the sliced, blanched cabbage down the centre of the swede purée.

10. Now create a cabbage-and-swede sausage by rolling the edge of the cabbage over and easing it over and over with the muslin until you have one long cylinder encased in muslin. Twist the ends of the muslin and tie securely with string. Fix with a couple of other lengths of string tied round at strategic intervals.

11. Carefully place this in a roasting pan. Pour in the stock. Cover with foil. Place in the oven pre-heated to 180°C/350°F/Gas 4 for 20 minutes. Lift out.

12. Take off the muslin carefully; it is pretty fragile. Cut into slices.

I would be persuaded that blackberries make the best version of this pudding of all, had I not had my friend Jane Lewis's mulberry summer pudding, which is positively imperial in its colour and flavour. But, as very few of us have access to unlimited quantities of mulberries, blackberries do very nicely. I can't remember whether it was my mother or my granny, who was tremendously greedy, who first thought of slathering the outside with whipped cream, but it filled me with unholy joy then, and still does. My contribution to the evolution of this dish has been the hazelnuts. A clever touch, I like to think.

1kg blackberry
100g caster sugar
lemon juice
8-10 slices of soft white bread, preferably thinly cut
285ml whipping cream
1tbsp icing sugar
50g hazelnuts

1. Sprinkle 600g of the blackberries with 55g of the sugar and lemon juice and leave to macerate for several hours.

2. Whizz the rest of the blackberries and the sugar in a blender or food processor. Strain through a sieve and keep the juice.

3. Line a basin with the bread, overlapping slightly and pressing together to form a seal. Fill up with fruit. Cover the pudding with another slice or so of bread.

4. Place a plate on top and a weight on top of the plate. Leave overnight or all day in the fridge. Unmould onto a large plate and pour the blackberry juice that you have kept very sensibly over all the pudding.

5. Whip the cream and icing sugar until it is stiff.

6. Plaster the outside of the autumn pudding with
    whipped cream.

7. Crush the hazelnuts coarsely and toast lightly in a frying pan
    before sprinkling the bits all over the cream.

Beer Zabaglione with Coffee or Chocolate Ice Cream

Glace de chicoree avec sabayon de la bierre – I can taste
Ghislaine Arabian's masterly pudding at Laserre still. And
she served it with a glass of chilled bierre blonde. I went
off into the night chirruping like a nightingale. Serve this poured
over really good coffee or ice cream.

8 egg yolks
50g caster sugar
240ml Arran Blonde or Leffe Blonde beer

1. Place all the ingredients in a bowl and place the bowl in
    a water-filled saucepan small enough so that the bottom
    of the bowl does not rest on the bottom of the pan.

2. Bring the water gradually to simmering point, beating the
    mixture with a whisk all the time.

3. When you have the warm, airy, velvety, fragrant mass,
    it is time to spoon it over the ice cream and serve it.

7. for ten or more
– the more the merrier

On my fiftieth birthday I cooked lunch for all the members of my immediate family. There were 33 of us in all. I made bollito misto with salsa verde and my saintly sister-in-law, Dilou, made her benchmark lemon tarts. We drank a lot of Barolo and it was a very, very happy occasion.

However – and there was almost bound to be a however – my small rump of the great gathering were left eating bollito misto in various forms for days afterwards. In my enthusiasm I had calculated my portions on the basis of what my brothers, sister and I had been able to eat about thirty years earlier (which was a lot), and sort of assumed that most of the others would do the same. Sadly, the passing of years had taken its toll on our capacities and much else besides.

Once you get beyond a certain number, I don't think the business of cooking matters much any more. I don't mean you shouldn't care. It's just that whether you're cooking for ten or twenty or thirty is almost immaterial. The effort involved is pretty much the same. You just know it's going to take a long time. Gauging quantities is a bit haphazard, but it's far better to have too much than too little. And make sure you have enough pans, large enough pans, and dishes or plates to serve off before you start. It's a bit late when you're already under way.

It's not something you're going to be doing very often. Nor is it likely to be a last-minute deal. So give it some thought. Go into training. Don't be too proud to use help if it's offered. And if it all goes according to plan, you won't have to do the washing up.

❧ a piece of cake ❧

Fennel and Olive Marmalade

OK, so strictly speaking it isn't a marmalade, but it remains a very toothsome spread on grilled bread all the same.

1kg fennel
250g stoned dried black olives
8tbsp sherry vinegar
1tbsp tomato purée
extra-virgin olive oil
salt and pepper

1. Slice the fennel very thinly.

2. Fry gently in 4tbsp olive oil until soft and golden. Add the olives, tomato purée and sherry vinegar and cook very gently for about an hour. If it looks like drying out, add a little water.

3. Whizz half to a pulp in a food processor. Mix the unwhizzed and the whizzed parts together and season.

Ricotta and Pesto Spread

Not really a recipe at all. But a good idea.

500g ricotta
5tsp pesto

1. Stir the pesto into the ricotta and spread onto thin crostini or savoury biscuits.

Pickled Herring

Stevie Lewis is a grand cook. So is his wife, Jane, come to that. It makes visiting the Lewis establishment a reassuringly convivial business. It's always good to know that you are going to be properly fed. This is one of the great S. Lewis dishes. He tends to make it in industrial quantities. You get your obedient fishmonger to provide you with the fillets. Once pickled, you never have to worry about light lunches, easy suppers or nifty nibbles until it's time to do another batch. Make sure, of course, that you get nice, fat, very fresh fish to start with.

Stage 1 – Salting
500g salt
1kg herring fillets

1. Scatter half the salt on a plastic or some other non-reactive tray.

2. Place the herrings on it.

3. Scatter the rest of the salt on top.

4. Leave overnight or for 8 hours to draw out liquid and tauten the texture. Judging the time is quite tricky, but it is better to undersalt them.

5. Wash off the salt very thoroughly.

Stage 2 – Pickling
250g caster sugar
150ml white-wine vinegar
1 dsp pickling spices
1 tsp peppercorns
2 large onions
2 bay leaves
salted herring fillets from above

1. Finely chop the onions.

2. Put the onions and all the other ingredients except the herring into a non-reactive pan. Bring to the boil. Simmer for 2 to 3 minutes. Cool.

3. Place the herring fillets in a container of some kind and pour the marinade over them. Leave in the fridge for at least 5 days. They will keep for up to a month in this state.

Stage 3 – Eating
250g crisp apples (Granny Smiths or Coxes)
150ml single cream
1 tbsp Dijon mustard

1. Of course, you can eat them just popped onto a slice of rye bread or crispbread, and very lovely they are too. Or you can slice them up into bite-sized chunks, mix them with the apple (peeled and thinly sliced), cream and mustard and have them like that. Or – well, use your imagination.

Potted Pigeon

Potting seems to have gone out of fashion. I'm not sure why, because it's a good deal easier than making patés and terrines. Or perhaps no one makes those any more, either. Anyway, potting is a great old English method of cooking, and lends itself to all manner of game in particular, although potted beef, potted ham, potted crab and, of course, potted shrimps all have their place on the larder shelf.

5 carrots
3 onions
1 tbsp juniper berries
½ dsp coriander seeds
225g butter
salt and pepper
6 pigeons
1 pig's trotter
6 rashers of bacon
2 sticks celery
120ml white (or ordinary) port
bunch of parsley and chervil mixed

1. Quarter the carrots and onions.

2. Crush the juniper berries and the coriander seeds and mix with half the butter. Season with salt and pepper. Put a knob inside each bird.

3. Put them into a casserole along with the celery, carrots, onions, pig's trotter, bacon and port. Make sure all the meat is covered. Add a little more white port, or even water, if you have to.

4. Bring to simmering point and cook gently for 1½ hours.

5. Cool. Pour the juices through a sieve into another pan and reduce by half.

6. Pull the pigeon meat off the bone and shred it.

7. Remove the bones from the pig's foot and chop finely.

8. Put all the meats into a bowl and season and mix.

9. Chop the herbs and mix with the meat. Pack into a terrine dish or individual ramekins.

10. Pour the reduced cooking juices over the meat. Cool.

11. Melt the rest of the butter and pour over the meat. Chill.

12. Serve with bread and a salad.

Spaghetti with Johnny's Souped-up Salsa di Pomodoro

There isn't much to beat pasta when it comes to feeding huge numbers, particularly if a large percentage of them are children. All you have to do is find a pot large enough. You can't cook large amounts of spaghetti in a small pot. You need lots of water. I've specified 1kg of pasta, because 100g per head is the classic proportion. Get good-quality pasta and don't drown it in sauce. You are supposed to be able to taste the pasta as well as the sauce.

1 kg or more dried spaghetti

Basic Sugo
1 large onion
5 cloves of garlic
2-3tbsp olive oil
several leaves of basil
1 large tin of tomatoes (or 2 tins of tomato pulp)
1 bottle of tomato passata
4tbsp extra-virgin olive oil

1. Slice the onion very finely (on a mandolin if you have one). Peel and cut up the garlic.

2. Heat the olive oil in a pan. Add one clove of garlic, fry until it begins to colour and then discard.

3. Add the onions and fry very gently for 5 to 10 minutes, covered.

4. Add some of the basil leaves, tomato pulp and passata. Cook gently for 30 minutes, partially uncovered.

Souping up
1-1½ dried peperoncino chillies
lots of freshly grated Parmesan, to serve

1. Chop up the peperoncino, the other garlic cloves and basil leaves finely. In a second pan, heat some more oil. Add them to the oil and cook on a very low heat until the garlic is brown.

2. Then add the sugo above and cook it all together for 5 to 10 minutes. Add the remaining basil leaves, finely chopped.

The pasta
1. Boil in lots of salted water. Make sure the water is well salted. The point of this is that if you salt the water properly, you won't have to add salt later on.

2. When you drain the pasta, keep half a cup of the cooking water to swirl it around in to stop it from sticking.

3. When you serve it with the sauce, make sure there's a bowl with lots of freshly grated parmesan ready to hand.

Sugo con Carne

I love this recipe because it's so practical and so thrifty. The tomatoes keep the meat moist and help render it to tender succulence. In return the meats give some of their flavour up into the sauce. You can use the sauce with a pasta first and then eat a slice or two of the meats with a salad afterwards.

2 large onions
5 cloves of garlic
2-3tbsp olive oil
500g beef (e.g. shin or brisket) in one piece
500g pork (e.g. shoulder) as above
2kg fresh tomatoes or 2 large cans tomatoes
1 bottle of tomato passata
salt and pepper

1. Chop the onion and garlic.

2. Fry gently in the olive oil until translucent.

3. Place the meat on top, then quarter the tomatoes and put on top of the meat along with the passata. Season with salt and pepper.

4. Bring to a simmering point and cook very gently for 3 to 4 hours.

On page 225 you'll find instructions on how to make sausages, but I'm not sure they are suitable for this recipe. You need something a bit spicier, with a bit more clout. Toulouse sausages or Merguez would do a treat.

1kg butter beans, preferably fasolia gigantes
2 large onions
2 sticks of celery
125ml extra-virgin olive oil
2x396g tins of tomatoes
2tbsp tomato purée
4 cloves garlic
2tsp dried oregano
salt and pepper
2kg continental sausages

1. Soak the butter beans overnight. Drain.

2. Turn on the oven to 170°C/325°F/Gas 3.

3. Bring a pot of water to the boil. Pour in the beans and boil for 30 to 40 minutes, until they are well cooked but not mushy. Drain.

4. Grate the onions and chop the celery.

5. Heat the olive oil in a casserole or heatproof dish. Add the onion and celery and fry gently until coloured gold.

6. Add the beans, tomatoes, tomato purée, garlic and oregano.

7. Season with salt and plenty of pepper.

8. Grill the sausages, then add them to the beans, slip into the oven and bake for 30 minutes.

My family comes from Lancashire, so we have very particular views on this, as do most Lancastrians, who tend to be as opinionated on hotpots as Irish men and women are on the matter of Irish stew. For the record I have not included oysters, although there is a school of thought that insists they should be there. To my mind, the kidneys are far more important.

15-20 middle neck lamb
(or better still, mutton) chops on the bone
75g dripping
1kg onions
1.5kg potatoes
15-20 kidneys
1 litre lamb or chicken stock
salt and pepper

1. Preheat the oven to 190°C/375°F/Gas 5. Trim excess fat from the chops.

2. Melt the dripping in a pan, and brown the chops on both sides. Set to one side.

3. Slice the onions finely and stew in the dripping until soft. Peel and slice the potatoes quite thickly.

4. In the crock/casserole, place a layer of potatoes, then a layer of chops, then a layer of onions, then a layer of kidney slices. Season and repeat until all the ingredients are used up, taking care to finish with a layer of potatoes (peel and slice a few more if you need to).

5. Pour in the stock. Brush the top layer of potatoes with any remaining dripping.

6. Cover with foil and then the lid of the crock/casserole. Place in the oven and cook for 2 hours. Remove the lid and let the top go brown and crisp – 20 to 30 minutes should do it.

Red Cabbage

And with your Lancashire Hotpot you can have this, although technically speaking it should be pickled red cabbage. If you're a stickler for authenticity, drop the port and cassis. The port and cassis bring a certain sweetness to the dish, offset by the vinegar, and help to keep the red colour. This is best cooked the day before, and is a classic veg for pork, too.

115g smoked bacon
115g carrots
1 onion
2tbsp duck fat, pork fat or butter
1kg (or thereabouts) red cabbage
225g tart apples (Bramley or Granny Smith)
2 cloves
salt and pepper
2tbsp red-wine vinegar
170ml port
2tbsp cassis

1. Cut the bacon into thin strips about 4cm long by 5mm wide. Slice the carrots and onions very thinly and fry very gently in the fat or butter along with the bacon for 10 minutes. Do not let them brown.

2. Slice the cabbage leaves very thinly, discarding as much of the stalk as possible.

3. Add to the pan with the other vegetables and the bacon and stir until well coated with the fat and slightly wilted – another 10 minutes.

4. Peel and thinly slice the apples. Add to the pan, along with all the remaining ingredients.

5. Bring to a gentle simmer, pop a lid on the pan, and cook very gently for 3 hours. Check from time to time that it isn't drying out. If it is, just add a little chicken stock or water.

Carrots and Pickling Onions in Beer

Just a lovely dish to have around.

10 large carrots
75g dripping
40 pickling onions
4 bay leaves
½ tsp coarsely ground pepper
1 bottle of bitter – Anchor Steam or Coniston Bluebird
120ml chicken stock
salt

1. Slice the carrots thinly.

2. Heat the dripping in a pan and cook the carrots for 5 minutes over a medium-high heat, until they just begin to wilt.

3. Add the remaining ingredients and simmer over a medium heat until the carrots are tender, about 15 minutes. Season according to taste.

Buttered Spring Greens

Greens as a vehicle for butter. I remember one prominent food writer, who shall remain nameless, having three helpings of this.

1kg spring greens
500g butter
salt and pepper

1. Wash and slice the greens, discarding the bigger bits of stalk.

2. In a saucepan melt half the butter and add the greens. Let them stew very gently for about 40 minutes.

3. Turn off the heat, and let them cool. You will find that, mysteriously, the greens will absorb all the butter.

4. Repeat the following day, and the same miraculous conversion takes place.

5. Don't let them cool this time. Season and serve.

Baked Pears with Sultanas, Pine Nuts and Honey

A change from baked apples.

10 (or more) not too ripe pears
150g (or more) sultanas
150g (or more) pine nuts
100ml (or more) any old honey
100g unsalted butter

1. Turn on the oven to 190°C/375°F/Gas 5.

2. Take a thin slice off the bottom of each pear and core them.

3. Plug the hole through the middle of the pear with sultanas and pine nuts. Don't worry if they won't all go in.

4. Put the stuffed pears onto a buttered baking tray and scatter

the remaining sultanas and pine nuts about them.

5. Pour honey over each pear and pop a knob of butter onto each.

6. Slide the tray into the oven and leave it there for anywhere between 5 and 15 minutes. This will depend on how ripe your pears are to start with. You need to be able to pierce them easily with a sharp knife.

7. Serve with buttery honey juices. And cream?

❧ no sweat ❧

Stuffed Focaccia

This should be the colour of ripe wheat on top and crisp, with the inside white and springy with a fat seam of filling running through the middle. I first ate it in Calabria. I've been eating it ever since. It's perfect for big help-yourself lunches or picnics. Of course you can make the filling of whatever you've got ready to hand. (NB, the lard. It should be pig fat – strutto – but that's hard to get hold of here. They never tell you that the true diet of the Mediterranean – in Southern Italy, Sicily and Spain – contains large amounts of pig fat, and mutton fat if you happen to live in North Africa. All the pastries are made with it.)

1kg focaccia dough (1kg plain flour, 50g fresh (or 25g dry) yeast,
500ml warm water, 1tsp salt)
115g softened lard
10 hard-boiled eggs
500g spicy sausage, cut into rounds (preferably sopressata)
400g fresh pecorino, finely sliced
1 egg, beaten
lard

1. Mix the focaccia dough in a bowl. Work until smooth and elastic. Move to a warm place and leave to rise for 2 to 2½ hours.

2. Put the dough on a work surface. Pull open in middle and punch down. Add the lard. Knead until the dough is elastic and silky. Put back in the bowl and leave in a warm place to rise again for another 2 hours.

3. Roll out half the dough to cover the bottom of a round tin oven dish greased with lard.

4. Cover with the hard-boiled eggs, sausage and pecorino.

5. Cover with the rest of the dough and bind the two parts with half the beaten egg. Prick the surface with a fork and brush with any remaining beaten egg.

6. Bake at 180°C/350°F/Gas 4 until golden brown.

Smoked Haddock, Mussel and Fennel Stew

Smoky fish, sweet mussels, aniseedy fennel. Divine combination. Handsome, too, the blue shells of the mussels sticking up out of the creamy liquor. I like mussels a lot; they're very generous with their juices.

1kg undyed smoked haddock
285ml double cream
1kg mussels
2 onions
600g potatoes
3 fennel bulbs
55g butter
150ml white wine
salt and pepper

1. Poach the haddock in the cream. Cool and flake the fish.

2. Clean the mussels, throwing away any that float or won't close.

3. Chop the onion finely. Peel and cut the potatoes into smallish cubes.

4. Cut each fennel vertically in half and then cut each half into four vertically. Trim out the feathery green bits and keep to one side.

5. Melt the butter in a casserole. Add the onion and stew until soft, about 20 to 30 minutes. Add the fennel and half the wine, and stew until soft – 20 to 30 minutes.

6. Add the potato cubes and stew for another 10 minutes.

7. Meanwhile, pop the mussels into a saucepan, pour the rest of the wine over them, clap the lid on and put them over a high heat until they are open.

8. Strain the juices into the casserole with the fennel and potato.

9. Add the haddock and the cream in which it was cooked, and return to the heat for 5 minutes.

10. Add the mussels, either in their shells or out. Sprinkle the feathery green bits of the fennel over the top.

Big Game Stew

A bit of a winter warmer, or autumn warmer to be precise. It represents a grand cleaning out of a deep freeze (I always tend to buy game in bulk when it's cheap, freeze it, and then find I'm a bit oversupplied). Of course, you can vary the meat constituents. Venison would go nicely, or hare.

100g dried porcini mushrooms
2 carrots
2 red onions
225g unsmoked bacon
1 sprig rosemary
4 sprigs sage
4tbsp extra-virgin olive oil
2 pheasants, 2 partridges, 4 pigeons, 2 rabbits
1 pig's trotter
1 bottle cheap port wine
2tbsp tomato purée
575ml game or chicken stock
4 cloves garlic
peel of an organic orange
55g butter
55g plain flour
salt and pepper

1. Put the dried mushrooms into lukewarm water to soak.

2. Chop up the onions and carrots.

3. Put them into a casserole along with the bacon and the herbs, garlic and orange peel.

4. Heat the oil in a frying pan and brown the game (having cut up the rabbit or hare). Do this in batches.

5. As the meat browns, move it to a casserole. Season it as you go.

6. When you have finished frying all the meat, pour a glass of the port into the frying pan, scrape up all the bits sticking to the bottom and reduce the vinegar to about a couple of tablespoons. Pour into the casserole.

7. Add the rest of the mushrooms and their water, port, tomato purée and stock.

8. Simmer until the meat is tender, 60 to 90 minutes.

9. Taste. If it's not concentrated to your liking, pour off the liquid and boil down until it is.

10. Melt the butter in a saucepan. Add the flour and cook until the mixture starts to turn brown. Add in some of the cooking liquids and stir until it becomes quite stiff.

11. Beat into the stewing liquid. Simmer for a moment or two until the liquid thickens.

Boiled Leg of Mutton with Salsa Verde

Your main problem with this recipe is finding a pan large enough to hold the leg. It does have to be pretty enormous. You can sort of braise it in a roasting pan covered in foil. You can, of course, roast it, very slowly, for hours (3½ hours at 150°C/300°F/Gas 2), basting along the way. If you are a stickler for tradition, you will prefer caper sauce, but to my way of thinking, this salsa verde hits the spot even more resoundingly.

The mutton
1 leg of mutton (approx 3.5kg)
2 onions
1 turnip
2 sticks of celery
2 leeks
2 bay leaves

a bunch of celery
2tsp peppercorns

1. Trim off some of the surface fat from the mutton, but not too much.
2. Place the leg in a pan large enough to hold it. Cover with water. Bring to the boil and simmer for 30 minutes, skimming off any grey gunge that floats to the surface.

3. Add all the other ingredients. Bring back to the boil and simmer for 3 hours or even 3½ hours, depending on its size and nature.

4. Now it is ready for the carver's art, the plate and the sauce (see below).

Salsa verde
4 hard-boiled eggs
8 anchovy fillets
12 gherkins
2tbsp capers
2 sticks celery
4 cloves garlic
1 very large bunch of parsley
peel of 1 lemon
extra-virgin olive oil

1. You can cut everything into a thin dice painstakingly by hand, which, as a true kitchen artist, you ought to do.

2. Or you can bung everything except the lemon peel and the oil in the food processor, and give it a couple of short whizzes so it is finely chopped. But not mush.

3. Then add the olive oil, as much as you feel appropriate to make a sludge but not a slush – say about 115ml. Grate in the lemon peel.

'Matty, please can you help,' said the voice at the end of the line. 'The lady who was going to help cook for all these people who are coming to stay the week after next has run off to the West Indies. Do you know anyone who I can find to take her place?' What could I do? Naturally I volunteered my services. She was dubious at first, but as she had no better Plan B, I was drafted in, and this was one of the dishes I served up. To rapturous appreciation, I may add.

3 pink grapefruits
3 oranges
125g unsalted butter
2tbsp peanut oil
6 pork fillets
250ml white port
285ml pork or chicken stock
150ml white vermouth
salt and pepper

1. Turn on oven to 190°C/375°F/Gas 5.

2. Peel the grapefruit and oranges until there is no pith left. Cut out each segment from between the supporting walls.

3. Melt 115g butter with the peanut oil in a large frying pan or, better still, sauté pan.

4. When foaming, brown the pork fillets, 2 or 3 at a time. When brown, put them into a roasting pan.

5. When all the fillets are browned off, pour off the butter and deglaze the pan with the white port.

6. Boil for a few seconds, and pour over the fillets.

7. Add the stock, cover with foil and pop into the oven for 15 to 20 minutes.

8. Pour off the cooking liquids into a pan, add the vermouth and reduce to a tasty level.

9. Add the bits of grapefruit and orange plus any juices collected during their excision from the surrounding walls.

10. Reheat gently, whisking in the remaining butter.

11. Slice the fillets into rounds and splash the sauce over them, making sure everyone gets a fair helping of fruits.

Shin of Beef Braised with Porter

I cooked this for my mother, aged 91, and her friend Meg, aged 92. They liked it. I hope you will, too. Of course, I've scaled up the quantities a bit. You can get porter in most offies and supermarkets these days. Use a stout if you can't find it.

3kg shin of beef
750g carrots
2 large onions
50g beef dripping
3 sticks celery
1 star anise
2 bay leaves
25g plain flour
peel of 1 organic orange
2 bottles of porter
salt and pepper

1. Chop up the beef into large chunks (or small ones if you like).

2. Slice the carrots, the onions and the celery all quite thinly.

3. Heat the dripping in a large casserole. When it is smoking, add all the vegetables, turn down the heat and fry until the onion is soft.

4. Add the meat. Conventionally you would now brown the meat, but I can't for the life of me think why. The beef never browns properly, the fat burns, the cooker is covered with fat spatters and all for what? So, add the star anise and the bay leaves and then the beef. Season.

5. Dust the flour over everything and stir it all round to make sure it coats everything.

6. Add the orange peel and pour in the porter. Bring gradually to simmering point, and cook for at least 2 hours.

7. Turn off the heat, and leave to cool overnight.

8. When you come to reheat the next day, check the taste and seasoning. If the sauce doesn't have enough oomph, strain it off and reduce it until it does. Pour it back over the meat and simmer for another hour.

Skillet Cornbread

Originally designed to go with the 9-hour turkey (see page 223), it will go equally well with any game or poultry.

300g streaky bacon
250g coarse cornmeal
75g plain flour
3tsp baking powder
1½ tsp bicarbonate of soda

300g sweet-corn kernels
600ml buttermilk
2 large eggs

1. Pre-heat the oven to 200°C/400°F/Gas 6.

2. Slice the bacon into short, narrow strips and fry in a 30cm skillet to leach out as much fat as possible.

3. When they are just beginning to crisp, take out the bacon strips but leave the fat where it is.

4. Mix all the dry ingredients together. Add the bacon and the sweet-corn kernels. Mix some more.

5. Beat the egg into the buttermilk and add that. Mix until just combined. Do not overwork. If it looks a bit dry, add a splash or two more of buttermilk.

6. Heat the bacon fat in the frying pan until smoking and pour in the mixture. If you don't have a skillet, use a roasting tray in the same way.

7. Pop the skillet or tray into the oven for about 30 minutes, until the surface is crisp and light brown and a knife plunged into the centre comes out clean.

Dilou's Oreillettes or Bugnes

This recipe and the next one were the fruits of my mother's nintieth birthday. We all made something. Dilou, whose full name is Marie-Odile, is married to my eldest brother, James.

500g flour
100g chilled butter

3 eggs
warm water
salt, if you are using unsalted butter
(not needed if you're using salted butter)
vegetable oil
granulated sugar

1. Put the flour in a bowl. Grate in the butter. Mix lightly with
    your fingertips.

2. Beat the eggs, add them and mix in thoroughly.

3. Add the water and a little salt if necessary. Form the pastry
    into a ball and work it hard for about 10 minutes. It should
    be quite smooth and silky.

4. Cover the dough and chill for 2 hours.

5. Cut the dough into 4. Roll out each piece as thinly as
    possible. Lightness is the hallmark of a great oreillettes, and
    lightness comes from thinness.

6. Cut each thin piece of pastry into strips 15cm by 5cm. Make
    a light slash or slit in the middle of each.

7. Heat 2-3cm depth of vegetable oil in a frying pan until the
    oil is almost smoking.

8. Fry a few of the oreillettes at a time for 10 seconds or so until
    golden brown.

9. Drain on kitchen towel. Sprinkle with granulated sugar.
    Cool. Keep in an air-tight container if you're not wolfing
    them down right away.

Lawrence's mum is Mary, married to my younger brother, Johnny.

400g finest dark chocolate
150ml double cream
50g butter
50ml Grand Marnier
50g ground almonds
50g madiera cake crumbs
100g cocoa

1. Put the chocolate and the double cream in a bain marie.

2. Bring the water gently to the boil until the chocolate
    has melted.

3. Add the butter and whisk hard for 2 minutes until creamy.

4. Gradually add the Grand Marnier and then the cake crumbs
    and the ground almonds.

5. Leave the mixture to cool in the fridge for 4 hours at least.

6. Take the truffle mixture out of the fridge and form into
    irregular small balls. Or irregular large balls if you like.
    The number of truffles you make will depend on how
    big you make them.

7. Roll in the cocoa and chill again in fridge, preferably overnight.

❧ making an effort ❧

Borscht

A big soup for big numbers. Borscht always looks splendid. It's the colour, of course, and the promise of richness, earthiness and the things lurking in it.

1kg beetroot and four more beetroot
1 celeriac
2 parsley roots
6 carrots
4 leeks
1 onion
4 beetroots
10 black peppercorns
2 allspice
1 bay leaf
85g dried mushrooms
1 glass red wine
juice of 1 lemon
salt and pepper

1. Start by making the beetroot stock. Roughly chop the root vegetables, except the beetroot, and the onion. Peel and slice the beetroot thinly. Cover with plenty of water.

2. Cook the vegetables along with the black pepper, allspice and a small piece of bay leaf for 30 minutes.

3. In a separate bowl soak the dried mushrooms in 2 cups of water.

4. Pour the vegetable and mushroom stocks through a sieve and mix together. Throw the cooked vegetable away.

5. Peel and grate the other 4 beetroot into a saucepan. Add the soaked mushrooms.Pour the red wine over and add the appropriate amount of vegetable stock. Heat the borscht until it starts to boil, but not more.

6. Season with salt and pepper and the lemon juice.

Nine-hour Roast Turkey

This may seem preposterous, but once you've tried it, there will be no going back. It simply produces the best roast turkey you will ever eat – assuming, that is, you start off with a decent bird. Ruthie Rogers, no less, told me she had tried it out. 'My chefs told me it would never work,' she growled. 'Best turkey we ever had,' said her husband, Richard. 'And I don't like turkey.'

Let's deal with the hard part first. You have to buy yourself a meat thermometer for this. And you have to invest in a good bird. Nothing can turn a broiler turkey into something fit for the plate. I use a 5-6kg (12-14lb) bird to feed 10, which goes rationally, with enough cold to be useful and not too much to get boring. If you have to cook a larger bird, you may have to cook it for longer. But not to worry. The principle remains the same.

1. Set your oven to the lowest possible setting. I have a slow setting on mine, which brings the temperature in the oven up to about 100°F.

2. Place the turkey in the roasting pan on its side, one thigh upwards. Add a little water to the roasting pan, and place it at the bottom of the oven.

3. After 3 hours turn it over, so the other thigh is uppermost.

4. After 3 hours more turn it breast down. (Incidentally, you

rotate the body because the legs and thighs take longer to cook than the rest of the bird, so it needs more exposure to a higher heat. This is less of a consideration if you have a convection oven, in which the heat is more consistently spread.)

5. An hour before you want to eat it, take it out of the oven. Turn up the oven to maximum heat. At this stage the turkey will still look much as it did when it went in, i.e. not very appetising.

6. So turn the turkey breast upwards in the classic position. Rub a little butter all over the skin and sprinkle with salt. Pop it back into the now-hot oven and roast until well tanned all over, basting from time to time. This should take 15 to 20 minutes.

7. Turn the oven off and let the turkey rest until you want to eat it. That is all you have to do.

8. Well, almost . . . You do have to take its temperature at various times, let's say when you're turning it over. The idea is to bring the bird's internal temperature very slowly to 62-65°C. This keeps in all the internal juices, keeps in all its flavour, and stops it getting tough and dry. In short, it makes the most of the turkey. No calculations of so many minutes at one temperature, and then so many minutes at another. No worry about overcooking or undercooking. No hovering, no worrying, no hassle. If you want Christmas dinner, put it in at midday or thereabouts. If it's Christmas lunch you fancy, bung it in just before you go to bed and check it when the kids come and bounce on your bed with their stockings.

9. If it goes a few degrees over 65°C, don't worry. If it doesn't look as if it's going to make 62°C just jack up the heat by 15 degrees or so. You may lose some of the juices along the way

as the fibres tighten up, but it will still be a well-succulent bird. Just keep monitoring the internal temperature. That's the important part, because if you bring a piece of meat to 65°C, and hold it there for 15 minutes, you will have killed off all the pathogens. It's as well to put the thermometer probe into the breast at the thickest point, and the thigh, too, and also in that area where the thigh is tucked up close against the main body of the bird. As long as they're all at 65°C, you're away, to do the rest.

Sausages (making them)

Mention sausages to anyone you like, and a smile will appear on their lips. Sausages are the great, universal, classless food. Everyone loves a sausage. You can't not. And there are still many fine sausages about. They're about the last great regional craft food still made on a regular basis. I spent so much of my life in search of the Ultimate Sausage, that I thought I ought to have a bash at making my own. They aren't the Ultimate Sausage – yet. But I will keep working at them. Still, I think the principles outlined below are a good place to start.

Meat
5kg pork
1kg back fat

Good sausages start with good ingredients. I get the pork from Andrew and Deborah who farm just over the hill near Minchinhampton. Their pigs are Tamworth–Gloucester Old Spot crosses. You can meet them as they wander around the farm, hairy and white with black botches or hairy and russet; Tamworth, the russet ones, give the flavour, while Gloucester Old Spot give sweetness and fat.

There's no need to use fancy cuts. Shoulder, belly and cheek are best; but definitely no ears, nose, tails, glands or bits and bobs.

And speaking of fat, I add about 1kg back fat to 5kg meat. But fat is good. It carries a lot of flavour and helps keep the bangers moist while they're frying. And if you cook your sausage properly, long and slow, most of the fat will leach out.

Casings

There is a splendid company called Natural Casing Co Ltd who send out casings by post. There are pig casings, sheep casings, beef runners, beef middles and beef bungs. I get 23 metres of hog casings which are enough to make 9kg of sausages. They are packed in salt, which means the ones you don't use can be kept for the next batch. They are not exactly sightly until stuffed with sausage meat. I make a rough guess about how many I'll need per batch, and soak them in cold water for half an hour or so until needed.

Seasonings
50g fine sea salt
5g white pepper
3g mace
5-6 cloves garlic

Seasoning poses radical questions. I use fine sea salt, freshly ground white pepper, ground mace and garlic. I have given exact measurements, but seasoning sausages is such a personal matter. Meat is an organic substance. Its characteristics vary from animal to animal, and so from batch to batch. In theory, each batch needs to be seasoned according to its needs. Except, of course, you don't know what its needs are. I like to add mace, too. This is the classic spice for British sausages, but you have to be dead careful how you add it. In tip-top condition, it is extremely perfumed and penetrating, so go easy. Finally, garlic. Garlic has a particular affinity with pork, bringing out the natural sweetness and flavour of the meat, but, like mace, do not use too much. It shouldn't dominate, so I add 5 or 6 large cloves per 5kg, mincing them up with the meat. Of course, you can add anything you ilike – leeks, parsley, sage, chilli, wine, whatever, but I am waiting until I have perfected Fort's basic banger before exploring more exotic fields.

Rusk/Breadcrumbs

To rusk or not to rusk? Not, in my view. Very definitely not, in my view. Your average British butcher will then tell you that a British banger is not a British banger without a healthy addition of rusk or rusk substitute. This is gibberish. There are plenty of Continental sausages which have nothing to do with filler. I do use dried bread, which I feed into the mincer from time to time along with the meat, but only as a means of preventing the mincing screen from becoming clogged up with sinew and fibre. I may get through 150g of it on a 5kg batch. So my sausages are, to all intents and purposes, 100% pure pork.

Equipment

There are big-time sausage-making machines, but as a rank amateur I put my trust in the mincer and sausage-making attachments for my trusty Kenwood Chef. This machine has made at least 30kg of sausages over the last couple of years, and while I can see the day when I may require an upgrade, that day has not yet come.

Process

1. Feed the meat, fat and bread through the mincer on a medium screen, letting the minced meats fall into a large basin.

2. Add the seasonings.

3. Make quite sure the mixture has been thoroughly amalgamated, mixing it thoroughly with your hands.

4. Now it's time to change the attachments on the Kenwood

Chef and get ready to fill the skins. This involves fitting one end over the projecting nozzle and feeding the rest of the casing after it, like massaging a condom onto a penis.

5. A flick of the switch and the minced meat begins to extrude into the skin.

6. Be careful to switch the machine off before you get right to the end of the casing, or a lot of the mince will extrude into space. Also, you need a bit of slack at either end if you are going to squeeze the meat down the casing to fatten it out and then put in a twist every 3-10cm or so.

7. And if you are a snagger neophyte like me, you'll then tie a short length of string between each length to make sure they stay as links and not relapse back into a single link.

Ilaria's Mum's Cantuccini

Another marvel from my mother's ninetieth birthday. Ilaria is going to marry George, one of Johnny and Mary's sons. She comes from Emilia Romagna, possibly the greediest region in Italy.

250g unpeeled almonds
150g caster sugar
100g vanilla sugar
2 eggs
250g plain flour
1tsp baking powder

1. Turn on the oven to 170°C/325°F/Gas 3.

2. Chop or crush the almonds roughly.

3. Beat the eggs and the white and vanilla sugars together in a bowl. Sift in the flour. Mix thoroughly. Add the almonds and baking powder.

4. Turn the mixture out onto a lightly floured surface. Roll the mixture into a sausage shape about 4cm across and cut into 6 equal parts.

5. On a nonstick sheet, press each of the bit of cantuccini dough into a flat round circle with your hand. Each disc should be about 1cm thick.

6. Bake the discs for 15 minutes. Turn up the oven to 180°C/350°F/Gas 4 for a further 10 minutes.

7. Take out of the oven and cut into strips 1cm wide while still hot. Leave to cool in a dry room until crunchy. The longer you leave them, the crunchier they'll be.

8. Serve with vin santo, although they were also very good with the beer, believe it or not.

Mother Fort's Brandy Snaps

And my mother's own contribution. Place a very large bowl of whipped cream beside a pile of these so that your guests can do their own filling.

100g golden syrup
100g butter
100g caster sugar
100g plain flour
2tsp ground ginger
4tbsp brandy

1. Turn on the oven to 170°C/325°F/Gas 3.

2. Pour the golden syrup, butter and sugar into a saucepan.

3. Place over a moderate heat and stir gently until all the ingredients have melted. Off the heat, sift in the flour and ginger and mix well. Add the brandy.

4. Place separate teaspoonfuls of the mixture on a well-buttered baking tray or a baking tray lined with silicone paper or, best of all, one of those wonderful nonstick space-age sheets. Make sure the mixture has plenty of space around it as it will melt and spread up to 12cm across.

5. Bake for 8 to 10 minutes. Cool for a couple of minutes.

6. Grease the handles of several wooden spoons with butter.

7. Lift the cooked biscuit off the tray with a palate knife and roll it round the wooden spoon handle. It takes a little practice to get this right, so it might be a good idea to make double the mixture.

8. Hold the brandy snap until cool, just a minute or so, and then put it to rest on a wire rack. If the biscuits become difficult to roll, warm them again ever so slightly until they soften.

index

and chesnut 192-3
red 207-8
sweet and sour with pork kebab
and carrot salad 26
white cabbage salad 37-8
with pheasant and white wine 103-4
cantuccini, Ilaria's Mum's 228-9
caper:
    lemon and celery sauce 87-8
    lemon dressing 29-30
    mayonnaise 124
    potato salad with 123-4
caponata 91-2
carrots:
    and chestnuts cooked in masala 126
    and pickling onions in beer 208
    and white cabbage salad 37-8
    chicken with elderflower and
    117-18, 132-4
    salad 26
cauliflower, crusted 60-1
cavalo nero with garlic, chilli and
    breadcrumbs 48-9
chestnut:
    and carrots cooked in masala 126
    and chocolate sauce 186-7
    ballotine of savoy with swede
    and 192-3
chicken:
    breasts in almond and lemon sauce
    151-3
    cold 123
    grilled breast, aubergine and chillied
    tomato 70-2
    korma 7
    livers and lettuce with a warm soft-
    boiled egg 24-5
    marinated breast with kohl rabi,
    carrot & white cabbage salad 37
    sausage with pistachios 145-6
    slivers with rocket 32-3
    spiced roast 45-6
    stock 27, 40, 51, 55, 56, 65, 78, 85,
    101, 110, 150, 152, 161, 167, 168,
    185, 192, 206, 208, 213, 216
    stuffed lettuce leaves 138
    thighs with sorrel and shallots 89
    with elderflower and carrots
    117-18, 132-4

chickpea:
    and fennel salad 47-8
    and pasta soup 119-20
    cod, roast with chickpea
    and vegetable stew and pesto 167-9
Chlwodnik, Adam Gebel's 159-60
chocolate:
    and chesnut sauce 186-7
    ice cream 195
    Lawrence's Mum's truffles 221
    soufflé with mars bar 113-15
cider:
    cheese 'n' ham on toast 28-9
    pork chops in carrots and 56-7
    potatoes 165
    salmon with broad beans, pancetta
    and 130-1
    sauce with duck roast and rillettes
    potatoes 104-8
coco bean, garlic and parsley soup 51-2
cod, roasted with chickpea and vegetable
    stew and pesto 167-9
consommé de vin au fruits 154-5
coucous, stuffed courgettes with harissa
    and tomato sauce 58-60
courgettes:
    couscous stuffed with harissa and
    tomato sauce 58-60
    thyme, lemon and garlic spread 76-7
crab and parmesan crisp stack 98-9
cucumber:
    and prawn salad 121-2
    and sorrel soup 166-7

dressings 43-4
duck:
    breast and lentils 35-6
    breasts with figs and fig balsamic
    vinegar 67
    confit of legs 169
    eggs, watercress, potatoes and
    pancetta salad 42-3
    roasted with cider sauce and
    rillettes potatoes 104-8

egg:
    duck eggs, watercress, potatoes and
    pancetta salad 42-3
    chicken livers and lettuce with